The Bus Leagues Experience

Volume 2

Eric Angevine

Chris Fee

Scott Grauer

Michael Lortz

Brian Moynahan

Tamara Swindler

The Bus Leagues Experience

Table of Contents

Travelers & Fans

Writers & Broadcasters

Players

Travelers & Writers

The Bus Leagues Experience

James Dively
Bus Driver for the Brevard County Manatees

Here at Bus Leagues Baseball we take pride in our interviews. We've interviewed players, administrators, and front office personnel. But we've never interviewed someone who actually drove a bus. It goes without saying, but bus drivers are the backbone of the bus leagues.

During a recent series in Tampa, I caught up with Mr. James Dively of Travelynx, the company that drives the Brevard County Manatees.

You are the bus driver for the Manatees, correct?

Yes, I've been driving them the whole year.

Is this your first year?

Right.

How did you get this position?

They had another fellow who couldn't afford to be on the road that much with his family ties, so I just inherited the position. Plus, I do all the collegiate athletics too, so it just kind of blended in.

Is that just the colleges in the Melbourne/Viera area?

No. I do the University of Stetson, sometimes we do UCF [University of Central Florida], Brevard Community College, there's quite a few. Daytona State College.

Wow. And this is all for one company?

Yes, Travelynx. We have special buses, they are modified with airplane seats, we have Wi-Fi on there for them, and we have 110 volt receptacles so they can charge their phones and all that stuff. It's designed for them.

You said this is your first year driving the Manatees. So how long have you been driving total?

Seven years.

What made you get into driving buses in the first place?

I've retired three times. I was in the military for 20 years, then I put 20 years in with Westinghouse, then I got a little bored looking for something else to do, so I got into this.

How many miles do you think you've put on?

Millions? I don't know. I lost count.

What is your normal day, especially when the team is on the road?

We'll leave Brevard and go to the hotel. So normally, if we have a 7:00 game, we'll get to the hotel around noon. We let the guys relax, then they board the bus at about 3:30 and we bring them to the stadium. Once they are at the stadium, they do their stretching and all that stuff for a 7:00 game.

Basically, when I bring them to the stadium the game doesn't start until 7:00, it's more or less free time because one, it's kind of hot to stand around and watch them stretch. So I'll typically go back to the hotel, or go to Wal-Mart or the mall or something. Or even a movie maybe. Then I'll come back in the second or third inning usually when it cools down a bit and watch the rest of the game.
Afterwards, usually they go back to the hotel, but sometimes they want to stop at a restaurant. And that's pretty much it.

The Bus Leagues Experience

You are on the road for every Manatees game, so that's 60-70 or so games, right?

I don't have my schedule, but that's probably pretty close. This is the last big trip. We have been on the road seven days, Clearwater for three, and four here in Tampa. Next week we have three commute days, we drive up to Daytona for the game and come home. And then that's the end of the season.

What do you do when the team has a long road stretch? What do you do when you are already in town?

I have to bring them to the park and back to the hotel. So I'll usually catch the last half of the game, maybe from the second or third inning. When it cools down a bit. Then we go back to the hotel and start it over the next day.

Are you a big baseball fan?

I've grown to be. I'm a Pittsburgh Steeler fan. I kind of grew into baseball.

How does minor league baseball driving differ from driving around the college teams? Are the people different?

Well, there are some tough questions there. These guys, it takes a little while to get to know them. That was part of the first bus driver's problem. He couldn't connect with them. Once you get to be friends with one or two, by the time the season's over you know everybody by their first name and they know you by first name and you know each other pretty well.

Have you had any incidents, accidents, or exciting stories along the way this year?

There was one story, it's kind of colorful. One of the guys autographed one of the girls, he physically autographed her. She was a very attractive lady, and I am not going to tell you where he autographed her.

It turns out, she was an umpire's girlfriend. How bad is that? That was kind of exciting for a while. They figured he would have a zero batting average. I guess it was all a good joke.

Nothing much happens. They get a few sore muscles, pack them in ice, and they are back there the next day.

Do you have more of an appreciation for the players than you had before you started?

Absolutely. They are doing this almost seven days a week all summer long. I don't think they get but a day off every two weeks. It's got to take a grind on them. But they are really easy to work with.

Is driving a team one of those jobs people seem to envy?

Well, to be truthful, not really. Once I got it, one of the advantages is that I know what my schedule is. It's black and white. I know when I can schedule personal things and when I can't. So there is that advantage. Some people don't like to stay overnight because of family situations and family obligations. Whereas my children are both grown and I don't have to deal with that.

So your plan after the baseball season is to start driving the college teams?

I'm already driving the Stetson girls' soccer team. They have a good schedule. They play out of state. They go to North Carolina and Nashville.

Driving with these guys [the Manatees] there is a plus too, it's an easy drive. You don't have to drive any farther than Jupiter to the south or going west any farther than Clearwater. That's a 2 ½ hour drive max. Whereas if I get the other jobs, I have to drive 10 hours up to Nashville. And then sometimes, when those girls get there, they want to go eat or they want to go somewhere. And I am already past my limit for driving hours.

Do you get paid by the hour?

No. I get paid by the day, but the Department of Transportation limits you on how long you can be on the road. So if you drive 10 hours up to Nashville, you are out of hours. Sometimes they have a problem with that.

How do you stay awake when you are driving 10 hours? That's a long haul.

It is. Daytime driving is much easier than nighttime driving. I don't seem to get sleepy. Nighttime driving is a bit trickier. I tend to eat real light; stop every 2 ½ hours to find a rest area, drench myself in cold water and walk around; and maybe do an energy shot for the heck of it. But you have to do that. If you try to stay awake for 10 hours you'll wipe out.

What is your favorite Florida State League venue or city to visit?

With the team? I would have to say Clearwater. There is a lot to do there. Here [Tampa] there is a lot to do, but it's not bus friendly. At the end of the night, say you are back in the hotel by 10:00, where can you take a bus?

There are a lot of places by the Tampa airport, right?

Well, we are staying in the Sheraton and they have a shuttle bus that will take you anywhere in the local area. It will take you to restaurants, to the mall, to Wal-Mart. So that's a good situation.

That takes the driving off of you, right?

Exactly, and it's good for them too because they want to go to dinner, they want to go to lunch, they want to go to the places guys go, you know.

Are you held to the teams curfews as well?

No, not really. I don't even know what the team curfew is. I don't think that it is that rigid. A lot of guys bring their fishing poles and they will go fishing late at night or early in the morning. I lot of them like to fish.

You learn a lot about the players as well, right? What they like to do?

Oh sure, some of them like to go fishing. Some of them like to play blackjack at the casinos. Some of them like to play poker. And some of them, their girlfriends come too. Not on the bus, but they will follow the bus down. I have a procession behind me sometimes.

So no one else is allowed on the bus besides the staff and the players?

No. I think that is an insurance issue with the league, I don't know. Makes sense though.

Are you a frequent visitor to Space Coast Stadium for games?

Well, that's where we pick them up, but yeah, I've been there a few times.

You've become a fan of the Manatees now, right? Is there any one player you would say is your favorite, either due to his personality or because you enjoy watching him?

Scooter [Gennett] is pretty interesting. He is a little guy, but he gets a lot of base hits.

Any opposing player catch your eye?

Not really. I don't follow them that closely. Unless they get a hold of one and knock it out of the park.

So you said Clearwater is the best park for you to visit, but what is the best to see a game environment-wise?

I think the ballparks in Jupiter and St. Lucie are nice. They are a little more in the country. They are a little bit easier to navigate. I think they are a little greener, it seems like.

Space Coast Stadium isn't bad, is it?

No, it's not. This place here in Tampa isn't bad either. The hardest part is parking at the hotel. It's tough. You can't go under the awning because it's too low. That means you can't make the loop around. And if you pull in, then you have to back out onto the highway. And that's not cool.
In the daytime, I don't mind. I can make six or seven swings and get turned around. But at night, it's tough. Daytime driving is so much easier. Sometimes they want to go eat at Steak 'n Shake or something and that can be tough if there are any low trees or parked cars on the side of the road.

How tough is it overall to drive a bus that size?

It's not that bad on the highway. On the highway, it's just like driving a big car. But when you start getting into parking lots, and start getting into real heavy city traffic, you have to be one step ahead of what's going to happen next. You can't get yourself down any cul-de-sacs or anything.

How many different types of buses do you drive?

We have about six different buses. As a matter of fact, we will be getting 25 new ones in a couple of weeks.

Is the company here in Florida?

Used to be. They sold out to a company in Argentina. This company has a concept of setting up something similar to Greyhound, except high end. So far they have a route that goes from Miami up the turnpike to Orlando, up to Jacksonville then to Atlanta to Washington DC and then to New York. Another one goes from Orlando to Tallahassee to I think Atlanta. It makes the loop. I have stayed away from that because that's away from home a lot.

What is your most challenging city? You mentioned Nashville and Atlanta, are they difficult?

Atlanta is easy. If you go where we go to Kennesaw, Georgia, it's just outside of Atlanta. There are a couple of colleges out there that Stetson plays. They have a bus lane, you can fly 70 miles an hour right through the middle of Atlanta.

So you mentioned you would do this one more year. What's after that?

I am probably going to retire after that. The last of my children will be out of college.

Then what?

I don't know.

Do you hear the players talk about who is moving up and who is moving down?

Yeah, they talk about that all the time.

Do you ever feel bad for a player who doesn't make it?

Well, yeah, they cut one of them. We were out on the field somewhere, I think it was Dunedin, and they cut a guy. It really upset him. He had big ol' tears rolling down his eyes. All the guys were giving him a hug. That's tough. I guess they had someone who was injured and came back. So they had to make a hole.

With the college teams you are not going to see that.

With the college teams, I see them from their freshman year all the way until they graduate and they are gone. I see them grow.

So which do you prefer driving: the minor leaguers or the college teams?

It's tough to pick one over the other. There are advantages to both.

Do you have a favorite restaurant on the road? I know it is mostly their choice, but what is your favorite?

Well, they talk about the Minor League Steakhouse all the time. Are you familiar with that?

No.

It's McDonalds. It's their joke. We always get a laugh out of that.

--Originally posted September 5, 2011 by Mike Lortz

Tug Haines
The Casual Fan

Traveling baseball fan Tug Haines is visiting the Florida State League now. I caught up with Tug in Dunedin during last week's game against the Clearwater Threshers and talked to him during the game.

Who are you and why drive around the country watching baseball?

Ok, well, my name is Tug Haines. I'm a cranberry farmer for most of my life and a big baseball fan. I was raised a Phillies fan. I started getting into minor league baseball the last couple of years. I got really hot for it last summer and decided I wanted to spend the 2011 season driving around the country watching minor league baseball and writing a book about it. A book about the whole trip, not just the games, but all the crazy stuff I see on the road and the people that I meet and the food that I eat.

What is your trip going to entail?

I go to a town, I check into a hotel (hopefully near the stadium), I go to the stadium, watch the game, take notes, take a lot of pictures, go back to my hotel, write a couple of blog posts about it, check out the next morning, and drive to the next town. Then do it all over again and repeat until the middle of September.

Right now we are in Florida, where are you going next?

Of course, I have the schedule all planned out, but this is basically how it is going: I'm starting in Florida, bouncing around like a pinball from coast to coast in Florida, catching all the Florida State League games and a Southern League game in Jacksonville. My last day in Florida will be the 24th of April in Jupiter. Then I am driving a few hours north to Savannah, Georgia.

Then I'll be going to games pretty much every day. I'll have a day off here and there, but it will go Florida to Georgia to South Carolina. I am bouncing around from Georgia to South Carolina into Tennessee to Mississippi, all the way to Memphis. I am staying east of the Mississippi River.

Then it is down to New Orleans, up through Alabama, through Tennessee again, through Kentucky, into the Carolinas, up into Virginia, to West Virginia, to Ohio, back to Kentucky, into Indiana, then Wisconsin, back down to Ohio, Illinois, Indiana again, into Michigan, back through Ohio, New York, Pennsylvania, then I am taking a break. I have five days close to home in New Jersey. Then I'll be driving to catch the short season teams in the summer starting down in Tennessee, with the Appalachian League. And then from then on it will be Tennessee, into the Carolinas again, Virginia, West Virginia, Maryland, Delaware, Pennsylvania, New Jersey, New York, and then up to New England. I'll end in Portland, Maine before I go to the playoff games.

Then, after the playoffs are all done, I'm hopping on a plane from Philadelphia International to Albuquerque, New Mexico. On September 19 and 20th at the Albuquerque Isotopes stadium is the Triple-A championship game between the champions of the Pacific Coast and the International Leagues. They will be playing that one game Super Bowl of Minor League Baseball. Then I am flying home on the 21st.

That is quite a trip. So what are your total numbers? What's the total number of games you will be seeing?

At least 113 regular season minor league games. It remains to be seen whether I will be staying around for the whole series in Portland. I have that option. Then the playoffs. I am estimated at least 125 total games through 27 states and at least 20,000 miles of driving.

You said you were going to try to turn your trip into a book. Do you have a publisher yet? Or are you planning on doing the self-publishing thing? Can you give insight on those plans?

Well, the whole trip is self-funded. I had that all squared away, so there wasn't a whole lot of pressure to find a publisher before going. I'm shooting to have a publisher do it for me because it is easier. They have professional editors who can do it for you. I'm a hell of a writer, but I'm not perfect. I don't know if I have it in me to publish a book. I suppose I could if I had to, but the plan is to find a publisher.

Now I did some looking into literary agents and publishers beforehand, just for information on what they were looking for. And they were all looking for a proposal or a manuscript. Number one, you can't get a manuscript until the trip is done, and number two, I didn't feel like wasting my time on a proposal if I'm not looking for an advance. I don't need any funding. I figured I am going to do this whether anyone is interested in it or not.

Because at the very least, this is something that not very many people get to do.

I guess that's my long way of saying I'm going to try to get it published by a publishing house because it sounds like a headache to publish my own stuff, as you are probably well aware.

What about your friends and family? Do they think you are nuts or are they supportive of your trip?

They are very supportive, and they think I am nuts. But that was before I came up with this. When I came up with this idea, I told my father about it. He is my boss and when I was approaching him to get six months off of my job, when I was finished pitching it to him, he said that this was something I should have been doing a long time ago. They all know that I love to wander. They all know that I love baseball. They all know that I love to talk to strangers. And they know that I am good at getting into adventures and getting out of them unscathed.

So they are not surprised. They know the kind of person I am and they have all been extremely supportive.

You told me you have been getting a lot of support from players and front office personnel. Could you tell me a little about that?

I knew it was a special thing. It was exciting for me. I sort of kept it under my hat and kept it close to my vest. I started planning last June in 2010. I didn't really make the news public, I told a few of my close friends, but I didn't break to any of the readers of the blogs I write for or my Twitter followers that I was up to this. As soon as I did, all sorts of support came out.

When I started sending emails to front office personnel, I wasn't sure how it would go, asking for credentials, and all that. But they have been very welcoming; they are very good at their jobs in public and media relations. And it is something has captured a lot of people's imaginations. So everyone, from players to fans to front office personnel, has been very cool.

I've made new friends on Twitter through this that are involved in Minor League Baseball. My friend Jeff Perro is a clubhouse manager for the Birmingham Barons, and he has been making calls on my behalf, getting me on pass lists in other stadiums as well. Michael Schlact is very helpful as well. He is a pitcher in the independent Atlantic League, on the Southern Maryland Blue Crabs. He has spread it around and other players have caught on to that. Then there is Logan Bawcom in the Dodgers organization with the Great Lakes Loons. He is going to put me on the pass list in June.

The people that really appreciate the game, they've said "I'm going to live vicariously through you." And that's kind of the purpose of the blog, the Twitter account, and the Flickr photostream. Everything I see and hear and think about I try to put out there. Because not everyone can go on a trip of this magnitude and it's almost like they are in the passenger seat with me.

Is there any game or any player you are particularly circling the date and looking forward to seeing?

Bryce Harper – I hope I catch up with him. I don't think he will still be with Hagerstown by the time I get up there, but I hope he doesn't head down here (to the Florida State League) before I can see him. I hope to catch up with him in Syracuse, if not Hagerstown. Obviously, he is someone to see.

Other than that, most of the Royals – that Royals farm system is really fun to watch and I watched them quite a bit in Wilmington (that's one of my favorite teams). Most of the guys I know by face or by name without having to look them up are on the field right now playing for the Threshers because they were with Lakewood last year. Guys like Jiwan James and Jonathan Singleton – he is a beast. Also Sebastian Valle.

Now the plan is that you will be meeting Brian of Bus Leagues Baseball in New Hampshire, right?

Right, and Eric in Virginia.

Is it your car or is it a rental?

It is my car, a 2006 Honda Accord that I named Wanda McCord. I'm not one of those weird people that names cars, but the AAA app on my phone gave me the option to name my car so I gave it a name that rhymed. So it is my 2006 Honda Accord that I purchased from my sister in 2009. Right now it has about 165,000 miles on it. It's due for service in 600.

So do you think it's going to be a mess in your car by the time you are done?

It's a mess in there now.

Will you be sick of the road by September?

No. I really don't think so. I think I am going to be tired, I mean I am kind of tired right now. I think once I get into the rhythm of things, which I think I've kind of found. I think I've found a rhythm, but now that Minor League Baseball season has started, I have to adjust it. I had to adjust it for Spring Training, for the down time between Spring Training and the start of the season, and again with the Opening Day of Minor League Baseball. And I am adjusting it again for night games.

I am not only adjusting my life schedule, but also learning to adjust the settings of my camera. I'm learning to photograph night games and photography on the fly. I know nothing about the art. But I am learning pretty quick.

Anyway, I am getting off point. I think I am going to be tired and I think I am going to be glad to be home. But I think I am going to get that itch again next March.

Are you planning to do this again in 2012?

I don't if I am going to do this in 2012, but I am definitely going to do something in 2012. I'm kind of shooting for taking lessons in Japanese or Korean, becoming fluent in either of those languages, and doing something similar in 2014, touring the Japanese or Korean Baseball Leagues. Because if you want to see wacky fans, you go to Japan, that's all there is to it.

Finally, where can people find you and keep track of you throughout the season?

You can find me at CasualFan.org, you can find me at Twitter.com/TugHaines, or on Flickr at Flickr.com/Photos/CasualFan, and I am on Facebook at Facebook.com/TugHainesCasualFan.

--Originally posted April 16-17, 2011 by Mike Lortz

Joe Price
Traveling National Anthem Singer

If there's one thing that should be obvious about the group we've assembled here at Bus Leagues, it's that we like things that are a bit off-kilter. And what better fits that description than a college professor who is using his sabbatical from teaching to travel the country, singing the national anthem at minor league baseball games?

That's what Joe Price, a Professor of Religious Studies at California's Whittier College, is doing this season. Along with his wife, Bonnie, Joe is driving around the country in a 29-foot RV, singing the national anthem the way he feels it ought to be sung, and writing about the experience. Mike met up with Joe down in Florida, and when we realized he would be coming my way, plans were made for me to do the same. I caught up with the Prices on July 6, a rainy evening in Manchester. After the three of us spent some time talking, I turned the recorder on and spoke with Joe about where this idea came from, why he chose to sing at Minor League games, and what makes a good anthem performance.

(One more note: Mike made a huge contribution to this interview; having planned to do one via email, he had sent Joe a list of questions, but the busy schedule of life on the road had prevented them from being answered. Those questions formed the framework of my conversation with Joe, and a strong framework I think it was.)

Who is Joe Price?

I'm a lifelong baseball fan, Professor of Religious Studies at Whittier College, and an aspiring musician who years ago thought that I could basically sing professionally, perhaps. Then I decided it was more fun to sing avocationally than professionally and became an academic instead.

Where did the idea of singing the National Anthem at Minor League Baseball games come from? The idea of this trip?

The Bus Leagues Experience

I have sung previously at 20 Major League ballparks, over the last couple of decades, and so I'm known around campus as having the weirdest hobby of any faculty member. And a colleague several years ago read an article about a fan who was trying to see a ballgame in every professional park in a single season, and he was well on his way but still had a month to go. And so my colleague said, "Joe, you should sing in all of the ballparks." And I said, "Wrong."

But as my sabbatical leave approached, as my wife was getting ready to retire, I thought, what better way to see the country, experience the distinctions of each community, than to try to sing in all the ballparks, all of the minor league parks. And so a year ago I began to contact teams for preapproval to get them to work with me on a date, and more than a hundred agreed to work with me on a date.

In the end I didn't hear from about 20 teams. Every team that I heard from except one said, "Great, we'll work with you." And I wasn't able to work it out with about 10, 15 teams in terms of just the sheer scheduling. So I scheduled 109 ballparks, and this was number 62. I had one rainout and two that I had to cancel because of RV problems.

It was looking kind of dark before the game tonight. Have you ever had a situation where you've been warmed up, ready to go, and then they throw the tarp on the field and delay you and you have to wait?

Twice. Well, twice here. It happened at one of the Major League games, at Coors Field. I sang the night of the Fort Collins flood there in Denver. At Durham, 10 minutes before the umpires were to come out, they covered the field, then it rained for 2 ½ hours. They managed to get the game started at a little after 10:20, and I stayed and sang for the game. I was warmed up and ready at Potomac, at Woodbridge, Virginia, and there they had called the game because the field was unplayable. In Charleston, South

Carolina, there were 2,000 gallons of water in the left field corner. I watched them remove it and calculated the number of 55-gallon garbage cans that they filled to empty it. Two thousand gallons. But they got the game in, and I stayed and sang. And in State College, Pennsylvania, the night of Stetson Allie's professional debut, they had a 30-minute rain delay, but they let me stay in the dugout so I didn't care.

So you got to just hang out?

Yeah, yeah. Then they let me stay in the dugout for Allie's first inning, so I got to photograph it from the dugout's perspective.

How much planning went into this trip? Obviously, you say 100+ teams, and you started a year in advance...

I can tell you the hours. Before I sang the first anthem this year I had more than 300 hours of work in contacting teams, developing the schedule, purchasing and preparing the RV, taking driving lessons in the RV because I had never driven a 29-foot vehicle before. So all of the preparations directly related to the trip, before I ever got to a ballpark, more than 300 hours. So it was eight 40-hour works weeks.

That's another full-time job. Were you working, were you still teaching?

Yeah, I was still teaching. Obviously last summer I had a good bit of time during the last half of the summer, and then I would spend up to 4-6 hours a day during November contacting teams about particular dates that might work.

Now, where this is a sabbatical from teaching – is this something you then have to go back and do academic work on your trip?

I'll integrate some of this into my teaching. I teach a course on Sport and Religion, and the national anthem basically provides a kind of consecration of the field for the civil religion of baseball. And so that's part of what I focus on in that particular class. So this does have some bearing on my teaching. But I'm also writing a book on the national anthem for the national pastime as a direct product of the sabbatical leave, and so I'm expected to make progress on that. The blogging is intended to be basically a rough draft of that book.

So do you do other events outside of baseball, or is it pretty much baseball, and is that the reason why?

Baseball is the one that I focus on because baseball prefers a traditional rendition of the anthem. I also sing for academic convocations and processions. I sing the national anthem for college football games and collegiate basketball games, but the NBA and the NFL, they're not really interested in my very traditional, up to tempo, clear presentation.

One of the other guys that I'm sure you know about is Tug Haines. We've kind of been following his travels as well, and the thing that he's always harping on is the national anthem. He said he ran through a rough stretch recently where seven out of ten of them or something was just awful. So what is it that makes a good national anthem performance?

Starting it in the right key – a singable key, so making sure you've got a good sense of pitch, so I have the pitch pipe with me and every night I make sure that I've got it in the key that I'm warmed up to sing it in. I'll sing it in either of two keys. Tonight I sang it in a lower key because I didn't have as rich or a low register as I often have. But starting it in the right key, singing it up to tempo, not providing any embellishments, and clear articulation – making sure you know the right words and pronounce them clearly. That's why it is the "national" anthem and not a personal performance. If it's the national anthem it needs to be embraced by all.

The Bus Leagues Experience

Tug and I met down in St. Lucie, Florida, for a game. It's the only time our paths crossed, was in the first week of the season. But we've followed each other's treks.

Now you're stretching out a little more than he is, because he's staying east of the Mississippi. By necessity you have to go kind of criss-cross.

Plus I'm not doing every ballpark, and it matters that I have to do it on a particular night that I'm scheduled, so if it's rained out, I'm out of luck. Not merely because it's rained out, but because I've got something scheduled for the next night rather than the flexibility to flip-flop.

Are you scheduled pretty much straight through? I mean, how many days off do you have planned in?

I'm singing 11 out of 14 days, and I restrict driving to 300 miles a day on which I sing. Three hundred miles to get to a ballpark. I might have to drive after.

Is that difficult on your voice? Do you notice it by the end of a stretch like that?

More difficult on my voice would be something like tonight, talking for 20 minutes over the crowd, than the singing itself.

I'm sorry [nervous laughter].

You know, it's worth it. But that's more of a strain on the voice. Keeping hydrated is the other key.

So you mentioned that you've sung in a bunch of major league parks. What are your favorite major league parks and what are your favorite minor league parks to sing in?

Favorite major league park to sing in is Camden Yards. The acoustics there are superb. The setting within the crowd is

26

embracing. The ballpark served as the model for the kind of ballpark revisions that have taken place in the last 20 years. So that one's my favorite. Emotionally a favorite was singing at Wrigley Field because I went to grad school in Chicago and I saw a number of games from the bleachers and from other seats.

Minor league parks – I loved singing in Daytona, which was a very old ballpark, intimate, the fans sang along. I love that. So that was a favorite, Class A, old ballpark. The acoustics in Rochester were quite good. I enjoyed that ballpark. Let's see…Frisco, Texas, and Round Rock, Texas, outstanding ballparks with acoustics and the design of the parks. Most memorable is probably Albuquerque, because I sang there the day after Osama bin Laden had been terminated, and there was a community's richness in its reception of the anthem, and so I was interviewed by both TV stations, a couple of talk radio stations. There was heightened awareness and receptivity.

About the acoustics – I've noticed in some ballparks, they have the speakers in centerfield, some they have the speakers behind home plate. I had never noticed this before until I went up to upstate New York – how much of a difference does that make?

Huge. At some ballparks there's almost a second delay. Last night at Lowell I had to use ear plugs. At Richmond, it's absolutely wretched in terms of the acoustics. You can almost stick your fingers in your ears. At that point I basically have to keep a mantra going: "Whatever you do don't stop, whatever you do don't stop, whatever you do don't stop, don't listen, don't listen, don't listen…" Just letting it go from memory.

Have you ever had one where you've gotten tripped up on the words at all?

No. In fact, I've done the four stanza [version].

So we won't talk about it anymore then. I don't want to jinx you.

That's the most frequent question, and then somebody says, "I hope I don't jinx you." It's not a problem.

According to a blog maintained by his wife, Bonnie, Joe's trip ultimately covered more than 28,000 miles between April 7 and September 1.

--Originally posted July 17, 2011 by Brian Moynahan

Torianne Valdez
Dunedin Blue Jays Super Fan

As part of our efforts here at Bus Leagues Baseball, we try to interview every aspect of the minor league baseball experience. Through the years, we've talked to people on the field and behind the scenes, but this year we are also trying to capture the essence of the fan. Because Minor League Baseball is nothing without the fans, those people who spend their hard-earned dollars to support their local squad and maybe see a glimpse of the big leaguers of tomorrow.

A month or so ago, I realized I was seeing a lot of pictures from Dunedin Blue Jays games on my friend Torianne's Facebook feed. Although it is usual for friends to have pictures from a game when you have baseball in common, Torianne was posting new pictures almost every week. So of course, we had to meet up at a game and talk about the bus leagues.

This interview was conducted shortly after Game 1 of Round 1 of the Florida State League Playoffs on September 6th, 2011.

How long have you been going to Dunedin Blue Jays games?

It's only been a few months, I would say. Since Spring Training of this year.

So what makes you a super fan?

I attend pretty much all the games. I just like the atmosphere. It's a hometown feel. It's very family oriented and very fun.

Your brother works for the team, right? How long has he worked for the Blue Jays?

He has been here since January of this year.

Did you attend games before he worked here? Or did you start attending because he works for the Blue Jays?

I did not come here before he worked here. He did introduce us to the City of Dunedin and ever since then, we have been hooked and we keep coming.

I had a chance to meet your whole family at a game last week. Can you talk about them? Is it normal for everyone to show up for a game?

Yeah, our family is really into sports so they were super excited when my brother got this job. I have two little cousins who are probably even bigger fans than me. They have their certain spot near the dugout during every game. Some of the players know them and go straight to them with balls. So our whole family loves it and they all attend a lot.

Is the Dunedin aspect new to your family? Or have you all met at Rays games, Lightning games, and other events in the area?

It's kind of a tradition. My grandfather went to [University of] Florida, so we grew up going to Gator games together. He would bring us to Lightning games. We go to tons of games during the year. So this is nothing new. But the Dunedin part is new.

Is there a big difference between getting together at a minor league game and getting together at a major league sporting event or a big college game?

Minor league is more relaxed, laid back, and easy going. I think that's why my whole family likes coming, it's something fun to do on a Friday rather than all the hoopla of going to an NFL game or even a Rays game.

How would you compare the Rays/Tropicana Field experience to Dunedin?

Fan experience it's similar. They have a very family oriented atmosphere and it's laid back. I do like that this is outdoors, even though they have been rained out plenty of times recently. But I do like that it's an outdoor stadium.

Is your whole family from the Tampa area?

We cover every area of Tampa: Carollwood, Temple Terrace, Brandon, Valrico, South Tampa, and Dunedin. We don't have anyone in St. Pete, that's it.

Are you going to keep meeting up here next season? Is your brother returning?

He just got a full-time gig here recently, so he will be here for years to come, I'm sure. We've already signed up for season tickets for next year, so yeah, we'll be back.

Who is your favorite Dunedin Blue Jay?

I would have to say probably Brad McElroy because I won his jersey on one of the theme nights and I met him there.

I know you told me once that you worked for the Tampa Bay Lightning. How do the players there compare to the players here?

The only experience I had with the Lightning players was when we had giveaways. We had to take season ticket holders to meet them. But we rotated and I only got to do that one time. So I met one player only. But these players are a lot more hands on. They are more approachable. They talk to the fans after the game and they sign autographs.

Have you been to any of the other local parks: Tampa, Clearwater, etc.? How does Dunedin compare to them?

31

I've been to Steinbrenner Field and I've been to Clearwater, where the Threshers play. Both of those seem a lot bigger than Dunedin, but I think they are a little more well-known as well. I enjoy Dunedin. Maybe it's because I am loyal to them now. I'll choose them over the Threshers.

Are you a Blue Jays fan now?

I'm still a Rays fan, but as far as minor leagues, I'm with the Blue Jays.

So what are some of the things you like the most about coming to the ballpark here?

I would have to say, number one, is the friendly staff [laughs].

Which of course, includes your brother.

Yeah, but I don't think I'll count him. Kidding. They are all super friendly, helpful, and they engage you in contests.

Now is that something that has increased as you have been become more of a regular here? Would you say you are part of the Dunedin Blue Jays family?

Yeah, I have gotten to know the staff pretty well. And I think we are the official family of the Dunedin Blue Jays.

Does that include everyone: aunts, uncles, cousins?

Yeah, we are all pretty well known here now. And only after one season.

Did you go to any spring training games here?

We did. We went to a couple of them. I came to the game against the Rays.

I tried to go to that one, but it was sold out.

That was the only one I think I went to. My family went to a few others. It's a much bigger crowd. It's harder to sit right behind the dugout. Still, it's a fun atmosphere.

That's another thing about the games here, that it's general admission. So where is your favorite place to sit? Are you a behind the plate person?

I like behind the Jays' dugout. You are low and can still see everything. My family loves to sit up higher in the corner of the stadium and out of the sun. But behind home plate is not bad either. It's not bad for six dollars.

Dunedin won its first playoff game, 4-3, before dropping the final two contests of the season to eventual league champion Daytona.

--Originally posted September 12, 2011 by Mike Lortz

Craig Wieczorkiewicz
Midwest League Traveler

This has been a banner season for traveling bards of baseball. We've been enjoying reports from Tug Haines and anthem singer Joe Price, both of whom are touring vast swaths of the country in their summer travels. Craig Wieczorkiewicz is also putting some miles on his car this season, but he's focusing exclusively on the Midwest League, the Class A home of various Snappers, Hot Rods, Kernels, Lugnuts and Loons. He's chronicling his journey with lots of tasty photos and stories at The Midwest League Traveler. I caught up with Craig just before he headed out to take in a game in Bowling Green.

You're touring the Midwest League. What's so great about "flyover country", as some would have it?

One of the interesting things about this journey has been the opportunity I've had to explore the communities these ballparks are in. None are in major metropolitan cities, of course, but some, such as the Lansing Lugnuts and the Peoria Chiefs, are in medium-sized cities, while others, such as the Beloit Snappers and the Burlington Bees, are in smaller communities where there is a lot less to do during downtime away from the ballpark. From the start, however, I made it a goal to learn a bit about each community and find interesting things to do there, and I'll be sharing what I discovered in my book.

On your "about" page, you say that you might enjoy minor league ball more than MLB at times. That's a sentiment we can get behind, but we'd love to hear your reasons. What makes the Bus Leagues so great?

There are so many things that make the minor league experience great. In my opinion, it's a purer experience than watching MLB because the guys on the field are playing their hearts out in hope of moving up the ladder to the big leagues. They're doing that while making little money, and some of them are doing it in a foreign country where they basically don't know anyone who isn't affiliated with their team.

Fortunately for them, they are plying their trade in more modern facilities (in most cases) than they would've been 30 years ago, and despite the tremendous improvements made to minor-league ballparks, the cost is still very affordable for families and hardcore baseball fans who like to go to a lot of games without going broke in the process. And minor-league players are way more accessible to fans than major-league players are – even the minor-league stars who are projected to make the majors someday.

You write a lot about the stadiums you visit. How big of an impact does the building itself have on your enjoyment of the game?

It doesn't have an impact on my enjoyment of the game itself, because I honestly can say I love watching baseball anywhere, even in the crummiest ballparks. That's not to say I don't like the modern amenities in the newer stadiums, because I do; those things typically enhance the overall experience at a ballpark. But they really don't affect my enjoyment of the game being played on the field.

Each of us has a somewhat quirky favorite player lurking in our subconscious. Mine's Jim Eisenreich. Brian's is Kevin Romine. Who's yours?

Jarrod Saltalamacchia. He has the longest last name in MLB history, and it just happens to be 14 letters long like my last name.

We also admit our shameful prospect man-crushes here. Is there a young player out there you just can't wait to see at the major league level?

Dayton Dragons shortstop Billy Hamilton. He has tremendous speed, the kind that can be a game-changer. At last check, he had 79 stolen bases this season. *[Ed. Note: Hamilton finished the season with 103 stolen bases in 123 attempts.]*

OK, lightning round about your travels in the MWL:

Best stadium?

My best overall experience was at Parkview Field in Fort Wayne. Fifth Third Field in Dayton is a close second.

Best food item?

The prime rib sandwich at Dow Diamond is very tasty.

Best mascot?

Homer, the Peoria Chiefs mascot. He's consistently interactive with fans, regardless of attendance or day of the week.

Best prospect?

Several players come to mind, but I'll go with Kane County Cougars pitcher Greg Billo, who has dominated Midwest League hitters all season. *[Ed. Note: After the season, Craig asked to include Jake Marisnick in his assessment of top Midwest League prospects, noting that the Lansing Lugnuts centerfielder "probably was the best all-around offensive player in the league this year."]*

Best promotion?

After the Miami Heat lost the NBA finals, the Peoria Chiefs gave away free replica Heat championship rings. In other words, they gave away nothing that day. I also got a kick out of the racing eyeballs in West Michigan. Three people wear giant eyeball costumes for a nightly race, which is sponsored by a local ophthalmologist.

Craig attended 81 baseball games this season, 64 of them in the Midwest League. He reached his goal of visiting all 16 Midwest League ballparks when he attended a game at Eastlake, Ohio's Classic Park, home of the Lake County Captains, on September 1. He traveled over 18,000 miles this season, including a 4,000 mile trip to and from Florida.

--Originally posted August 15, 2011 by Eric Angevine

Writers & Broadcasters

The Bus Leagues Experience

Bruce Baskin
Baseball Mexico

Mike brought the blog Baseball Mexico to our attention a few weeks ago. We all have this strange fascination with the Mexican League, which is an official MiLB Triple-A league, but none of the league's teams are officially affiliated with big league clubs. Mike broached the subject in his interview with MiLB commish Pat O'Connor, but we're still mystified and intrigued.

Turns out, so is Baseball Mexico creator Bruce Baskin. He has felt the same pull. When I asked him via email if I could interview him for Bus Leagues, this was his response: "Sure, I'd be happy to answer your questions…Maybe in the process I'll come up with my own reason why I cover baseball as played in a country with a language I can't speak or write. Thank the Big Guy Upstairs for Google and Babel Fish translations (which sometimes need translations themselves)."

With that as your introduction, let's meet Bruce.

What is it about the Mexican League that caught your interest, and what keeps you interested enough to write a blog about it?

I've always been interested in the Mexican League. There's just this "mystique" about it…you'd hear about players who've gone down there to play (Negro Leaguers in the old days, former prospects and ex-big leaguers in modern times) as well as a large number of homegrown guys who spend 15-20 years playing there. Plus they have teams in exotic places like Veracruz, Yucatan, Puebla and Mexico City, so there was that draw, too. It seemed like baseball's version of Terra Incognita; you know it's there, but you don't know WHAT's there. There's a book called "Some Are Called Clowns" by Bill Heward, who wrote a diary of the 1973 Indianapolis Clowns (for whom he was pitcher-manager), and one of the chapters was about a ballplayer who'd spent some time in Mexico. I was 15 when I read it and it fascinated me.

40

As for the blog, it really started out in 2005 as a creative outlet in the form of a weekly column for the OurSports Central website. I was "between jobs" in radio and wanted something to do so I wouldn't go crazy. I'd covered the PCL for OSC in 2001 but I wanted to do something unusual this time, so I asked Paul Reeths, "How about cricket?" "No," he said, "no pro league in the USA." Then I asked about Japanese baseball: "Lots of guys go over there and quite a few players from there are coming here." "Nah," Paul says, "I'm really looking for sports leagues in America." Then I remembered the Mexican League and asked, "How about that?" Paul said since the Mexican League is a Triple-A minor league, that was okay with him so I started the Viva Beisbol column. The rest is more or less history.

Why do I keep doing it? I guess I like learning new things and six years ago, everything I knew about Mexican baseball could've fit in the two paragraphs above. Another reason is that (I'm told) there are a lot of people in Mexico who know who I am and are fascinated that a gringo takes their baseball seriously enough to write about it on a regular basis, so in a way I feel it's a role I've assumed as the Anglo voice of their game. Which is kind of cool.

Is there a team in the Mexican League that consistently rises to the top? A Yankees-type organization?

There are some well-run ORGANIZATIONS down there (Monterrey, Saltillo, Yucatan and Puebla are good ones), but the closest to Yankees would probably be the Mexico City Diablos Rojos. Their owner, Alfredo Harp Helu, is a very rich guy who is also very demanding...making the playoffs won't cut it because he expects pennants and he'll spend money to bring in players. A lot of similar qualities to George Steinbrenner, actually.

The Diablos don't necessarily have the best overall attendance (although they set a single-game record this year with over 27,000 on Opening Night), in part because Foro Sol was not designed for baseball. A new baseball-only facility is on the drawing board, but things move slow in Mexico and it may take time before it's built.

Mexican League teams aren't affiliated with big-league clubs. What's the appeal of playing there for a player who's not native to Mexico?

There are two answers, depending on which league you're talking about.

The winter Mexican Pacific League is a good place for prospects to get extra at-bats or innings (although the Caribbean Leagues in general have been hurt by the rise of the Arizona Fall League because MLB organizations are keeping top prospects home now). The MexPac is also good for players with minor or major league experience who are free agents wanting to audition for a spring training gig or show they're recovered from an injury.

On the other hand, the biggest draws the Mexican League has for non-natives are the decent paychecks (money for foreigners is comparable to most Triple-A salaries) and the chance for older guys to keep playing at a competitive level. Mexico is a lot nicer and safer place to live than a lot of people north of the border give it credit for (the drug war there has changed that dynamic somewhat, although visitors are rarely involved). Lots of players go there only intending to play for a season or two and end up spending several years because the people are nice, a lot of the cities are beautiful, the weather is warm and a Triple-A-level salary goes a LOT farther in Merida than in Memphis.

For that matter, is it a good road to take for a native-born player, since there's not a huge likelihood of getting to the bigs?

In a way, it's the ONLY road for a Mexican-born player. Here's how it works: Any good young prospect will have his rights assigned to a Mexican League team at a very early age (a good parallel might be if the NHL drafted Bantam-age players instead of a Junior league like the WHL). At that point, any MLB organization interested in signing a young Mexican player has to first negotiate with the LMB team that owns his rights first before negotiating with the player...kind of like when the Mariners had to give the Orix Blue Wave millions of dollars before even talking to Ichiro Suzuki in 2001. You might see guys like Luis Heredia signing with the Pirates last year, but it's expensive. Historically it's been a lot cheaper to sign multiple Dominican players at the cost of one Mexican, although that gap is closing.

The result is that a lot of young players are locked into Mexican League teams because MLB teams often find it a hassle to sign them.

Having said all that, the Mexican League is not a bad way to go for those players. The pay scale for domestic talent is lower than for foreigners, but the money is still a lot better than they'd be getting in other occupations. Not that it's fair, but it IS relative.

Have you ever seen a game in person? Is the atmosphere different than in the U.S.?

I went to two games in Mazatlan in December 2010, and the atmosphere is a LOT different than in the States. Many of the elements are the same: Music between batters and even between pitches, on-field entertainment between innings, mascots, vendors in the stands... Still, it's DIFFERENT. The music alternates between rock and various Mexican genres, the vendors are selling souvenirs as well as food or drink and the overall atmosphere is more party-like. If you've ever watched a Caribbean Series telecast, you get an idea, but it's really nothing like being there. In the States, teams try to manufacture fun for fans; In Mexico, the fans are already HAVING fun.

You say you have a following south of the border. Do readers from there ever send you photos or stories of their experiences?

I've been TOLD I have a following south of the border by a friend there who is very well-connected in baseball there. That's a little different than my experience, which has been to hear from an expat here or a baseball person there. As far as genuine response goes, I can't say I've had much of it. I'm pretty sure the teams and leagues do know who I am, but may not be sure what to make of me...it's not just me, though. Communication with teams and leagues is notoriously bad. I had an agent last winter asking if I could get the word out that his client (a former MLB player) was looking for work, and this was a guy who could've helped at least one team for sure. I try to stay away from that because, hey, I'm a writer, not a broker, but I gave it a shot in this case. No response at all. It's just how it is.

Who is the best player in the Mexican League right now?

Well, right now, I'd say Luis Terrero of the Mexico City Diablos Rojos is the best player this year. After 80 games, he's hitting .376 with 28 homers, 83 RBIs, 90 runs and he's 22-of-27 in stolen bases. It's a hitter's league, but those numbers just jump out at you. Of course, you've got entire teams hitting over .300...I think everyone in the Diablos' lineup hits over .300. Another one is Ruben Rivera, who's been playing for Campeche for a few years now and he's at .348/26/78. The impression I get is that he's really grown up the past few years since he was with the Yankees and has even become sort of an elder statesman of sorts. Willis Otanez, who used to play for Toronto and Baltimore, is a great batter down there. He's bounced around from team to team, but he's always put up good numbers. Then there's Japhet Amador of the Diablos...great big guy. He was in the Mets' training camp this spring. He's 24 and batting .406 right now. I think of all the native players, he might be the best bet to end up in the majors.

Among the pitchers, I'd have to say Andres Meza is the guy. He's got 10 wins and his ERA is 2.76, both best in the league. He's only 5-foot-11 and doesn't get a lot of strikeouts, but he's got good control...maybe two walks every nine innings. He's only 25 and is 35-9 since 2009. Meza can obviously flat out pitch. Joel Vargas of Veracruz has 10 wins, too, but I wouldn't quite put him in Meza's class. Danny Rodriguez of Saltillo is 26 and a lefty who got some attention last season with a great playoff run and the Rockies were said to be very interested, but he's really inconsistent and hasn't had a great year. A personal favorite of mine is Francisco Campos of Campeche. He's 38 now and another pitcher who isn't very big, but he's consistently a double-digit winner, his ERA is always under 4.00, and he gets lots of strikeouts. He's in the All-Star Game every year, and was the South starter this season. Campos has been around forever, but he keeps producing.

How popular is the Mexican League in relation to other sports like soccer?

It depends on what part of Mexico you're talking about. Soccer has definitely passed baseball in popularity in the country as a whole. The people running the LMF (Liga Mexicana de Futbol)have been very proactive in promoting their sport and getting games on TV for several years and it shows. Soccer games are well-attended and it's not hard to find a match on TV. Baseball hasn't done as good a job of reaching out to potential fans, although the president of the Mexican Pacific League, Omar Canizales, seems to "get" it. He's maybe the best exec down there. Baseball is still the favorite sport in the northwest states of Sonora and Sinaloa (where most ballplayers from Mexico seem to come from) and it's pretty strong in Veracruz, but it's a pretty distant second to soccer when taken on a national basis.

What is your approach to covering the league – do you do anything that's unique to your site?

I guess it sounds facetious, but just covering both leagues in English is what makes my site unique. Nobody else is doing it, which I find surprising. This is a nation along our southern border with 100,000,000 people (and millions more of Mexican descent living in the US), they've been playing baseball since the late 1800's, and the Mexican League does play a fairly high quality brand of ball with a lot of veterans who've played there for years and years. It's the closest thing to a classic pre-farm system minor league on the continent, yet there are several websites devoted to baseball in Japan but only mine to baseball in Mexico…and exclusivity hasn't made my site as well-visited as I'd like to see, that's for sure.

Beyond that, I just try to have fun while writing about baseball in Mexico, but with a sense of accuracy and respect, especially for the players. I'm pretty dubious about some of the owners and league officials, but never the players. The biggest frustration I have is in trying to verify something written in Spanish, which is a language I can't speak or understand verbally and am pretty weak in reading. I live in mortal fear sometimes of getting something REALLY wrong. Thank God for Google translations and BabelFish, plus I've got subscribers who are fluent in Spanish that I can check with if I'm still not 100% sure of something.

If you go to a Mexican League game, are there still hot dogs, peanuts and cracker jack? Inquiring minds want to know.

At the games I went to in Mazatlan, I don't remember seeing much American food. I DID have what may have been the worst hamburger I've ever eaten that I got from a vendor…you'd do better getting one of those 99-cent burgers that have been under a heat lamp for hours at a mini-mart. After that, I just stuck with a strict cerveza diet at the ballpark. Which reminds me of something.

I was in a private box the first game I went to in Mazatlan, which was very nice and we were well taken care of, but it wasn't the same. The next time I went, it was in the grandstand behind home plate with a Canadian couple I'd met. I was telling them who the players were and just trying to give them a general idea of what they were watching. Well, behind me, this local guy tapped me on the shoulder and handed me a beer he'd just bought. We didn't say a word because of the language barrier, but a smile, a nod and a thumbs-up can get a point across pretty well. Like I say, we'd never said anything, but he was just being a good guy and a good host to a visitor.

That might be the biggest reason why I write about Mexican baseball: It's as much about Mexico as it is baseball. I've written about a lot of different things over the years, but I've never felt the same sense of personal connection like I do with this.

--Originally posted July 6, 2011 by Eric Angevine

Clark Brooks
Tampa Blogger

One of the more interesting sports folks I've met since I moved to Tampa, Florida is local blogger Clark Brooks. Clark has been around Tampa sports since the mid-80's and has worked with nearly every professional sports team in the area. Although I have known Clark for a few years, after he told me recently that he got his start working for the Tampa Tarpons, Tampa's old minor league team, I knew he and I had to sit down for a chat.

So who is Clark Brooks?

Who is Clark Brooks? Wow. I am a writer. I do a lot of freelance stuff. I do a lot of self-publishing. My main professional gig as it pertains to sports right now is that I am a staff writer for RawCharge.com *(Ed. Note: a Tampa Bay Lightning blog)*. I have previously been involved with SBNation's Tampa Bay hub. I used to write for the Rays for a column called "Clark Calls It" for DevilRays.com, when it was the Devil Rays. I had a column for America Online called "Deep in the Cheap Seats", which was a Minor League Baseball column, back in the early days of AOL.

I also have a professional background working in sports for hockey, NCAA college sports, and Minor League Baseball.

Can you talk about your start in the Tampa sports scene, and with Minor League Baseball in particular?

I moved down to Tampa, Florida in 1986 from Michigan. I like to tell people that we were doing the bad economy thing before it was fashionable everywhere else. So I have been here since 1986, and the first job I got here was a part time staffer at the old Tampa Stadium with a concession company. At that time, right next door was Al Lopez Field, which was the home of the Tampa Tarpons, the Single-A affiliate for the Reds at the time, as well as Spring Training home for the Reds.

I ate dinner at a local Denny's and there were free tickets to a game right by the cash register. I thought it was the greatest thing ever that there were free tickets to a baseball game, so I snatched them up thinking they would go fast. I got to the game and saw that there were about 200 people there and quickly learned that Minor League Baseball was not a big draw in Tampa, Florida. But I enjoyed the atmosphere and I enjoyed the fact that I could sit wherever I wanted. I had great access – the equivalent of major league seats that would have cost around 30 dollars at the time I could sit in for free, or on a pay night, for only two bucks. And since it was right next door from where I worked, I would go there all the time.

Also, since I worked for the concession company, and since the Tarpons were kind of a Mom-and-Pop operation, which was still the case in Minor League Baseball back then when they had such things, we were frequently in the position of lending food prep equipment and that type of thing to the Tarpons for their use. And I got to know people in the front office and I wound up dating the assistant general manager and I was at the Tarpons game almost every single night.

I was 22 at the time, so basically the first people I met that were my age were ballplayers for the Tarpons. So I started hanging out with those guys. Up until the point that I realized they didn't have to be at work until four o'clock and I had to be at work most times at 8 a.m. So hanging out was kind of limited to weekends after I realized I couldn't hang with their schedule.

So it was just a good match for me, falling in with those people and meeting them, with me loving baseball and the proximity of the team being right there. I just kind of worked my way into the Tarpons family at that point.

And being that it was a mom-and-pop thing, that when people talk about the legendary days of Minor League Baseball where one day you are painting fence lines and the next day you are mowing grass and the next day after that you are cooking hot dogs, that's pretty much what I was doing. But I dug it.

I was wondering if you could tell me a little about the significance of the Tarpons to the community. Were they big here?

Well, they were an established team. They were kind of an institution in that they had been there so long. They played in Al Lopez Field, which was the namesake for Tampa's first Hall of Famer and the guy who put Tampa on the map as far as baseball is concerned. They had been a Reds affiliate since the '50s and Pete Rose played there *(Ed Note: The Tarpons were a Phillies team from 1957-1960 and a Reds team from '61 to '88.).* It was the kind of thing where everybody had been to a Tarpons game, but not everybody went to a Tarpons game every night. So it was kind of like an institution that people took for granted.

So they didn't draw very well?

No. And being that they were my first real exposure, I thought it was a Tampa problem, but after traveling around I found out that the Florida State League and baseball in general wasn't a really big draw.

And this was prior to the big boom that hit Minor League Baseball in about 1988 or 1989 when Bull Durham came out and the Carolina Mudcats came around and everyone took off with the quirky mascots and nicknames and Minor League Baseball was big all over the country. That boom never hit Florida, for whatever reason.

What happened to Al Lopez Field? Is that where Raymond James Stadium is now?

It is. The owners of the Tarpons, the Mick Family, Mitchell and Buddy Mick, two brothers, and they didn't have a lot of money and the Tampa Sports Authority was not real receptive in keeping

Al Lopez Field. They wanted the land the ballpark sat on for other considerations. At the time, a basketball or hockey arena was planned for Tampa – this is before the Lightning was a gleam in anyone's eye. Everyone saw the location as prime real estate and for lack of a better word they basically forced the Tarpons out of business.

They stopped maintaining the ballpark, they put minimal effort into upkeep, and the stadium deteriorated. Part of that is where the Yankees' complex is now, and was the Reds Spring Training complex. They let that deteriorate to the point where the Reds moved out. They let that go downhill to the point where the Reds moved out of Tampa and moved to Plant City. Conditions were so bad, the building couldn't be salvaged and they weren't going to put any more upkeep into it. Well, the same building is still there 20 years after the Reds moved out. It is a workout facility near the cloverleaf of practice fields – it's the same building. They just put work into it once the Yankees got involved.

So things got so bad and conditions got so bad, the field was a joke, and we didn't have a full tarp. We had tiny, six-foot sections of tarp that we had to cover bad spots with. We were fixing puddles with kitty litter. There was a pronounced lip coming off the outfield into the infield were you could physically see a hill. It was awful. I remember our screens for batting practice were chain link.

They tried to hang on as long as they could. Everyone was thinking that Major League Baseball moving to Tampa Bay was imminent. If you were the holders of a franchise, you stood to cash in, as the Major League team would have to buy out your rights for professional baseball in the area. So the Micks held on as long as they could hoping they could last until Major League Baseball expanded or moved to Tampa Bay and they just couldn't do it. Once Al Lopez was untenable and they couldn't get an agreement to go to the University of South Florida, they pretty much had to sell the franchise.

The Bus Leagues Experience

Baseball in Tampa Bay, you are talking about 1988 with the White Sox and 1989 with the Giants, right?

Right, and I think the Twins and the Mariners before that. They kind of flirted with the idea too. So at that point everybody was thinking a move was much more likely than expansion. Everybody thought the next time Tampa Bay was going to be given a team. And that was pretty much the climate for a long time in Tampa Bay.

So were there any future major leaguers that you may have hung out with while working with the Tarpons?

I was pretty good friends with Chris Hammond, who made it to the big leagues with the Reds, then went to the Marlins, then had a noteworthy comeback with the Braves after he was out of the game for a couple of years. Chris was a good guy.

The Tarpons really didn't push a lot of big leaguers through. A lot of big leaguers came through the other [Single-] A club in Cedar Rapids. But the Florida State League at the time was a pitcher's league and the Reds didn't have a lot of pitching prospects coming through.

What about Tom Browning?

Browning did, but he was before my time.

They had a club in '83 that had Tom Browning, Paul O'Neill, Terry McGriff, Tracy Jones, they had a pretty solid club in '83.

And Eric Davis would have been before that?

Yeah, and I don't think Eric Davis ever played for the Tarpons though. I think he went through Cedar Rapids.

We were the High-A club, but they put more prospects through the Midwest League for whatever reason.

Proximity to Cincinnati, possibly?

Could be.

You sort of mentioned this earlier, but could you talk a bit more about your day-to-day actions?

Well, I worked my regular job with the concessions at Tampa Stadium then head over to Al Lopez at night. It was like "Hey, we are shorthanded in the kitchen, so go in the kitchen and cook hot dogs."

There were a couple of Saturdays where I mowed grass. One of our ushers, an employee, lived down the street. I would borrow his push lawnmower and I mowed the infield with that one Saturday morning. I put out the screen for batting practice, I lined the field, I did PA announcing for a couple of innings, and I sold souvenirs. Basically, whoever was available was available to do whatever.

It wasn't departmentalized at all. I think there were maybe three full-time employees. There was the GM, the Assistant GM, and one other person working in the office. That was it. The rest were game day employees only. Even bat boys were actually boys, like Little League-age kids.

I don't think anybody gets by without a staff of at least five or six now. Plus interns, plus sales people. The idea of having sales people was a completely foreign concept.

So it was basically just tradition that drew people to the Tarpons games? Did they do any kind of marketing at all?

Well, they put out the free tickets at the restaurants and you could pick the free tickets up. One of the good things about the Florida State League is that teams are always sending their major league players down for rehab assignments. So occasionally you get a big

53

leaguer playing and people find out about it and they will come out for that.

We did promotions. We did giveaways. We did fireworks. Stuff like that.

Any promotions stand out?

From the Tarpons? Everything was always trade; there were some giveaways, but nothing crazy.

Have you been to any Tampa Yankees games and how does that compare?

Not a fan. First of all, I am not a Yankees fan. Secondly, Steinbrenner Field holds about 10,000 fans, which for a minor league game, especially when nobody draws, is way too big. And I don't get the minor league vibe there like I get at some of the smaller ballparks. It seems kind of sterile and cold and empty. They are not drawing any more than we used to draw with the Tarpons.

Do you have a favorite Florida State League ballpark, past or present?

I like the Lakeland ballpark. I also liked old Jack Russell Stadium in Clearwater. It was almost a copy of what Al Lopez Field looked like. The seats were real low, almost a foot or so higher than the field itself. That was the same as Al Lopez, which where the seats were maybe two feet or so above field level. Real intimate and real close to the action. You could sit right next to the dugout. The grounds crew at Jack Russell was amazing.

And yours was you.

Well, me and a few other guys. It wasn't just me. But I think the Tampa Sports Authority would only come out to mow the grass with a tractor like once a week. And the rest of the time we had to make due with a push lawnmower. Like I said, the Tampa Sports Authority basically ran that team out of town, the Reds and the Tarpons both.

You mentioned you worked for Mike Moore. Could you talk about that?

Mike was the GM at the time, from 1987 to 1988. Then he left and went to the National Association to become the president, which is now Minor League Baseball. It was known as the National Association of Professional Baseball Leagues at the time.

Could you tell us a little about working for Mike Moore?

Mike practiced what he preached. He would cook hot dogs and work the PA. Mike was a local Tampa sports legend before he got the job with the Tarpons. He was on TV with some of the old TV personalities in the '70s. He used to call pro wrestling in the area.

Mike just liked to do his job and not be bothered. He had a radio code – I don't remember what the signal was – but when the owners were there we were to give Mike a radio so he could hide in the tunnels and not have to deal with them. He loved the game but he was not into the "big timeness" of being in professional baseball. He didn't kiss the ass of dignitaries and he wasn't impressed by celebrities.

Did you stay in touch with him as he became President of Minor League Baseball?

Yeah, I kept in touch with him. I haven't talked to him in a while. He is retired now. I think he spends all of his time fishing. But yeah, I stayed in touch.

I actually married the girl I was dating with the Tarpons after Mike left. And he was the best man at our wedding. So we used to socialize with him and his wife.

You said you were married at home plate, right?

Yeah. Married at home plate at Al Lopez Field. Al Lopez was there. Which is very cool. My grandmother was swooning over him. That wedding was the last event at Al Lopez Field, as they tore it down the next month. And while Al was still alive, too. Which is basically an embarrassment of huge proportions.

How you let someone outlive their own monument is beyond me.

Any funny individual stories before we go?

Yeah, the last year we were with the Reds, we had a centerfielder named Steve Davis. He was one of the guys I hung out with. He was talking to a little kid before the game who had this little novelty glove. The kid wanted Steve Davis to use it in a real game. Davis knew he wasn't in the lineup that day, so he took the kid's glove and said, "Yeah, I'll wear your glove on the field."

Right about the fifth or sixth inning, Davis got put in as a pinch hitter and was told to stay in the game. So the guys on the bench told him that he had to take the kid's glove out. They told him that he promised so there was no way he could go out there and not take the glove. Davis objected, saying he couldn't go out there with a kid's glove, literally the size of his hand. But he took it out there and played centerfield.

Sure enough, a ball is hit to him.

He makes this long run and makes this amazing over-the-shoulder Willie Mays catch with this kid's glove on. Nobody knew he had this glove on except for the kid and the guys who knew he promised. The dugout is going nuts. Great play. One of the greatest plays of the year.

He goes back to the dugout and all he hears is that he was making a mockery of the game. They can't believe he wore that glove out there. They called him a clown. They were all giving him crap.

So that was kind of fun.

Clark's writing can be viewed at RawCharge.com and at his personal blog, Ridiculously Inconsistent Trickle of Consciousness.

--Originally posted August 1-2, 2011 by Mike Lortz

Jim Donten
Claw Digest

I always enjoy finding fan blogs of minor league teams. There is a passion needed to cover a team not too many fans know about. And if done well, an independent minor league team blog can quickly become the alternative voice for people looking for news on a prospect or on the team.

As I mentioned last June, there are few really good fan-based blogs of teams in the Florida State League (yes, the failed flotsam and jetsam is still out there). Last year, I interviewed Jeff Crupper of Threshers Nation. Shortly after I talked to Jeff, a new blog joined the scene: Claw Digest, a blog on the Charlotte Stone Crabs, the Tampa Bay Rays High-A affiliate out of Port Charlotte, Florida.

I emailed Jim Donten, webmaster and lead blogger at Claw Digest and asked him a few questions about his site..

What is Claw Digest and how long has it been active?

Claw Digest is a site I created at the end of the 2010 season. I wanted to create the site prior to the start of the inaugural season but a lack of time and experience caused the project to be put on the back burner. But then after last season, I took a leap and created the site. The site is a collection of news, stats, photos, and inside looks at the Stone Crabs organization as well as periodic updates on the careers of former Stone Crabs.

What is your blogging background and baseball fan background?

I have been a lifelong fan baseball fan. I grew up in South Central Pennsylvania going to Philadelphia Phillies, Reading Phillies and Harrisburg Senators games. I relocated to Florida after graduating high school in 1998 and lost interest in going to live games due to the abundance of things to do in Florida, however I still enjoyed watching MLB on TV. But a few years later, I took a special detail with my fire department for a fireworks shoot at Ed Smith Stadium for a Sarasota Reds game. The excitement of being back in the ballpark renewed that love of watching live baseball and we have been going regularly ever since.

I began my online work by combining my two favorite things, baseball and photography. I created a web gallery of photos of all the games and players I saw play in Sarasota through the Sarasota Reds and the Cincinnati Reds. These photos appeared on both clubs official websites and various blogs.

When the Rays moved to their Advanced-A affiliate to Port Charlotte, I switched alliances to the newly formed Stone Crabs who are just seven minutes from my house. During this time, I reached out to Rays Prospects and offered them the use of photos like I had already done for Reds Minor Leagues in the past. Doug Milhoan and I began a great friendship in the process and I eventually took up writing as well.

After two seasons of writing for Rays Prospects, I started Claw Digest. I still continue to write for both sites.

Why do a blog on the Tampa Bay Rays class High-A team?

I have been a season ticket holder for the Stone Crabs since the inaugural season and live less than 10 minutes from Charlotte Sports Park. I covered the Stone Crabs and the Florida operations for Rays Prospects for two years. Then last year I decided to branch out and provide a little more detailed coverage of the Stone Crabs and Claw Digest was born. It was an opportunity to incorporate some of my ideas that were too intense to do organization wide but were easy to manage at a local level.

The Stone Crabs are a relatively new team. How has the local response been to the club?

59

The local response to the Stone Crabs has been fantastic and I attribute that to the management of the club. General Manager Joe Hart and his staff do an excellent job of marketing the team in Port Charlotte and the surrounding communities. Their commitment to the community through public appearances and helping local organizations goes a long way in selling the image of the team. They have made the ballpark and organization very fan friendly through special events and it shows seeing how they led the league in attendance in each of their first two seasons. This is evident driving through town or walking through the stores when you see Stone Crabs hats and shirts on people and banners on building and cars representing the team.

Do you think the team benefits from having the Rays only an hour away?

I am not really sure there is much of a benefit from having the Rays being so close. I think the bigger benefit is that the Stone Crabs play in the Spring Training complex of the Rays. This allows easy access to first class playing and rehab facilities as well as having roving instructors visiting the club quite regularly. Because of the rehab facility, the Stone Crabs tend to have MLB players rehab with them quite frequently, including BJ Upton, Carlos Pena, Pat Burrell, Jason Bartlett, Scott Kazmir and more have spent time with the Stone Crabs in the past two seasons.

Who has been your favorite Stone Crab so far?

There has been a bunch of great players that have come through Charlotte in such a short time, it's hard to pick just one. One of my overall favorites has been Stephen Vogt. He had performed both on the field and off the field. He got hurt in 2009 and spent much of the season on the DL. During this time, he continued to help out with the team, helping coach and even appeared in a game as an umpire when the FSL ump was injured. In 2010 he made up for lost time by leading the league in hitting and then headed to Columbia for Winter Ball where his hot streak at the plate continued. Stephen was also big in the community and always volunteered his time to helping the club which led to him winning the 2010 Erik Walker Community Champion Award.

A few other personal favorites include Henry Wrigley, Tyler Bortnick, and Cody Cipriano. Wrigley provided a big bat in the Stone Crabs lineup and he led the Stone Crabs in home runs in 2010 despite being promoted to Montgomery mid-season. Bortnick is a hard-nose player that is a lot of fun to watch, he only spent a few games with the Stone Crabs last year but I am looking forward to seeing him play this season. Cipriano was another fun player to watch for the Stone Crabs, knocks the cover of the ball and comes through in clutch situations plus the ability to play multiple positions in the infield.

You saw Matt Moore last year. Thoughts on him?

Moore's performance on the mound was amazing. His started the year off slow but worked closely with pitching coach Neil Allen to refine his grip. He led the minors in strikeouts for two years in a row while lowering his walk-out rate. Moore had a bone chip removed from his hand during the off-season and is reported to be feeling better and throwing better. So if this minor adjustment will help avoid a slow start, the ceiling for Moore is unlimited.

You saw Tim Beckham last year. Thoughts on him?

Unlike a lot of other people, I have not lost faith in Beckham. He did not have a breakout season like predicted with the Stone Crabs but he faired average in a predominantly pitchers league. He was able to reduce his errors between 2009 and 2010. I witnessed Beckham make some spectacular plays at short with the Stone Crabs however I also saw him miss some what appeared to be routine plays. Better consistency will help round out his game and push him towards living up to the hype of being a first round pick with the largest bonus in franchise history.

Who should we keep an eye on this year?

The Bus Leagues Experience

A personal favorite of mine this season is Tyler Bortnick. This kid plays the game of baseball the way it was meant to be played. He gives 110% on the field and finds the way to make the play over and over again. He tends to fly under the radar amongst players in the organization but look for him to have a solid year with the Stone Crabs.

I am also interested in seeing how Jake Thompson does in his first full season. He was promoted to the Stone Crabs late 2010 and started two games for the Stone Crabs. But in those two games, his pitched 11 innings and did not allow an earned run while striking out six and holding hitters to a .059 average. I am eager to see if the Rays second round pick from 2010 will continue his success in the Florida State League.

Last year, the Stone Crabs played in the Florida State League Finals. How do you think they will fare this year?

The Stone Crabs have reached the playoffs in each of their two seasons in the league and I don't think this year will be any different. Under the leadership of Jim Morrison, the club has managed to make it back to the playoffs despite who is or is not on the field. He gets them to play as one and no matter what part of the puzzle is replaced, the team continues to function and win games. This is key with the revolving door that is minor league baseball. The lineup seems to be missing a big bat, but I think the players on this year's club will get it done with extra base hits and timely hitting rather than the big fly. Plus you have the strong pitching staff that like the two previous years will help lead the Stone Crabs into the postseason.

On August 23, 2011, Jim closed Claw Digest, noting that, "It has been a lot of fun and I really enjoy providing the stories, but it is time I focus more on my family." Five weeks later, on September 29, he reopened.

--Originally posted April 12, 2011 by Mike Lortz

Kurt Schweizer
Miami Minor League Baseball Historian

In an effort to continue exploring the history and impact of Minor League Baseball in Florida, I've been corresponding with Kurt Schweizer, unofficial historian of minor league baseball in Miami, especially the original Miami Marlins. With the Florida Marlins renaming themselves the "Miami Marlins" and moving into a new stadium in 2012, I thought it would be great to talk with Kurt and get his opinions of baseball in South Florida, and also learn a lot about the sport's history in the area.

Who is Kurt Schweizer?

Wow. No one has really asked me that before. Interesting question. To put it simply, I am a Christian, son, grandson, boyfriend, nephew, cousin, cat owner, writer, friend, bandmate, lyricist, drummer, photographer, student, history buff and sports fan.

You've been called one of the foremost historians of minor league baseball in Miami. How did you originally get into minor league baseball?

I take that as quite a compliment. But, it certainly didn't happen overnight. I'm from and have lived in Miami for the vast majority of my life but we lived in Lakeland for a short time when I was a kid. So, my dad took me to my first game at Joker Marchant Stadium in August of 1979 when I had just turned eight years old. My dad had always been into baseball a good bit from a fairly young age, but I didn't completely take to it right away. I liked it but I wasn't bitten by the bug just yet. But, that game planted the seed. Then, when we moved back to Miami, he and I started going to Miami Orioles games pretty regularly in 1981. And that was it for me. I have been almost obsessed ever since. (And some people would say it isn't actually almost.) We also were season ticket holders for the University of Miami Hurricanes baseball team for about 10 years, also starting in 1981. And I was one of the original season ticket holders of the Florida Marlins, but, somehow, it was the minors that really sucked me in and kept me.

When did you start getting into the history of the teams and the facilities you visited?

I had always been interested in history, in general, ever since I was a little kid. The Miami Orioles played at Miami Stadium which was a very interesting place to watch a game. It had a very interesting unique design and really reeked of history even though it, having been built only 32 years prior to my first visit, wasn't all that old, as we think of historic stadiums today, such as Fenway and Wrigley. But, it did already have an interesting resume, if you will, that included the Major League Orioles and Dodgers for Spring Training and the old Triple-A and Single-A Miami Marlins plus the Miami Sun Sox in the minors, as well as the short-lived Amigos of the ill-fated Inter-American League. And it didn't take long for me to start trying to learn about all that from whatever books I could get my hands on and from some of the old timer fans there. But, right away, there was something about it that sucked me in. I don't know exactly what it was but it had a really cool aura to it. It almost seemed like a haunted house. And it was so large and cavernous for a minor league stadium. Plus it held well over 10 thousand but typically wouldn't have any more than a hundred or so, on average, per game, for the minor league season, so I would have fun just roaming around sometimes and just checking it all out. I have never seen another minor league stadium quite like it and I have been to many. It was kind of like a ghost town, all within the confines of a single building. And that's something that's pretty interesting to a nine-year-old boy...at least it was to me.

Then when I was a freshman in college, I was in an elective class called "Skills and Practices in Baseball" which was right up my alley. There was some fieldwork but also a lot of textbook and classroom work in the class. For the term project I did a report on the entire history of pro ball in Miami, up to that point. And that research was pretty specialized. And since it was 1990 and pre-internet, as we know it, I had to get about 90% of the information from old local newspapers on microfilm at the library. It was very time-consuming, but was worth it. It even further sparked my interest in the history side of everything. Then I used that research as the basis for some articles that got published by the Fort Myers Miracle (formerly known as the Miami Orioles, Miami Marlins and Miami Miracle), in their programs, starting in the 1991 edition. But that first program article was more of a summary of the different Miami franchises and the different names used and Major League affiliations by year. Then, in 1998, while I was working for them full-time, I wrote a franchise history story in prose form for that year's Miracle program which got reprinted in several other editions, over the years, as well. And I ended up doing a lot of other stories for them, mainly relating to baseball history in some way.

What projects have you been involved with in regards to the history of Miami baseball?

There have been several, to varying scopes, over the past 20 years or so. Most of them revolve around the articles that I have written relating to the history of the Miracle franchise and for the Twins spring programs. But I have also written a couple articles for other projects and websites. There was also a fairly large feature story about Miami Stadium that I was interviewed for in The Miami New Times in 1996, which served as a catalyst for the PBS movie about the stadium that I was involved with as an interviewee, consultant and contributing photographer. There have been a couple other projects that I have consulted on, including ones for the Florida Marlins and Major League Baseball and with a couple museums. And on top of that I am working on a doctoral dissertation revolving around Minor League Baseball and Spring Training in Florida, which I hope to one day turn into a book. I also have a page on Facebook, relating to the history of the Miami Marlins and Minor League Baseball in Miami. I have some pictures I took, along with contributions from others, on that site and there are two fairly large galleries of my pics on two other websites.

What has been the reception to your projects?

I would say it's been pretty favorable. I haven't really had people beating down my door, but I have gotten a lot of emails from fans and even a couple from players, relatives of players, and staff, from all over the country (and even one from the UK), telling me that they enjoy my articles and pictures. So, I always like that. I also was contacted by Roy Firestone, whom had been a batboy for the Orioles in Spring Training when he was a kid. That was really nice. We've yet to meet in person, but he was also in the same PBS film as myself. And I am always happy to be asked to do various projects and writings here and there.

When did you start documenting the end of Miami Stadium?

Well, I knew, going back to about the early '90s, that its days were really numbered.

There was a fight to save it from demolition, that was led by a couple of the producers of the documentary and I was involved with that. But, that movement was not ultimately successful. So I was not surprised when I read in the Miami Herald that demolition had begun. That was in late May of 2001. I went there the next day and just started taking as many pictures as I could from every angle feasible. I got permission from the president of the demolition company to be on the property as long as I wore a hardhat and agreed to the assumption of risk for legal purposes, which I did. So, over the course of about the next two months after that, I went to the stadium about 3 or 4 days a week to document the demolition process. And even in the years prior to that, I got permission from the City of Miami Parks Department to take pictures of it several times and they were very cooperative with me on that.

When did you realize the end was near?

The first real sign was the Marlins moving out of there, in the middle of the 1988 season. Then when the Orioles discontinued using it for Spring Training after the 1990 season, I knew it was very likely just a matter of time. The baseball team from the downtown campus of Miami Dade College still used it through 1996 and I even went to many of those games, but I knew that team, alone, would not be enough for the city to justify keeping the stadium open. So, it was bought, I believe, in about 1999 by a housing developer. And then the clock started to speed up a bit on its death watch. So when the demolition finally started to occur a couple years later, I was still sad but not a bit surprised.

How important was Miami Stadium to the people of the area? What made it so important to baseball history in general?

It was important as it hosted not only Minor League ball from the time just after it opened in 1949 right up to 1988 but also Spring Training, from 1950 to 1990. It helped put Florida on the map for both of those things. And in Florida, especially, the two have generally been pretty intertwined. Plus that was and still is very important to the economy and tourism industry in the state. Miami Stadium was also used for many other events besides baseball, such as concerts and things of that nature, in addition to other sports. And from the purely historical perspective, there were countless Hall of Famers who played at Miami Stadium, either in a spring game and/or in a minor league game. On top of that, it had an innovative architectural design, which included the grand cantilevered roof that it became famous for amongst architects and some photographers.

Miami seems to get a bad rap in the baseball world these days. Why do you think that is? Have the attitudes towards baseball in South Florida changed?

Many people have wrestled with that question for a while. It's not an easy question to answer. There are many variables. But, I would say that Miami has, for over 70 years now, been primarily a football town, for college and then also pro. And, of course, we are one of only a handful of metro areas to have the big four major sports, but football is usually where most of the local sports fans want to put their entertainment dollar. But, baseball has always, I believe, been the favorite local participatory sport, which doesn't always translate into significant revenue for admission-charging teams. Another aspect, too, is that there are so many non-sports choices for people all over Florida from which to choose to spend their money. So, baseball, as a spectator sport, often gets left behind. But, the main way I have seen baseball in Florida flourishing is within Spring Training, which is, indeed, very closely tied to tourism. For the last 15 or so years that it was held there, though, attendance suffered during the spring at Miami Stadium, because the area that it was in was not perceived as being a safe place to go to anymore. I think that's a relative thing, but I could see where people thought that.

You made a comment on a website once that said you will never set foot in the new Marlins stadium. Why not?

That is a question that I am a bit hesitant to fully answer because I have several acquaintances and former classmates whom work for the Florida Marlins. I respect all of those people and I think they are very good at what they do and I don't want to insult any of them in any way shape or form. Having said that, though, I know that a lot of people in South Florida were not pleased with the way their ownership group went about securing some of the funding for the new stadium and I can see why some people have some hard feelings towards the Marlins about that. Also, for me, it has a lot to do with the demolition of the Orange Bowl and the way all of that was handled. Of course, my main interest related to sports is baseball history. But I am also a huge fan of football and its history. I think the fact that the Orange Bowl was torn down without any attempt at retrofitting it or preserving any part of its structure is almost a crime. I will miss the Orange Bowl almost as much as Miami Stadium. And I know a lot of people share that sentiment and many even more so than myself, I'm sure. Another important aspect that I think the Marlins and the city overlooked is the traffic infrastructure issue around the new stadium. Anyone who has driven to that area during rush hour will understand what I'm referring to. Of course, it wasn't a problem for the Dolphins and Hurricanes because the vast majority of their games were on weekends. But, I don't think that area's roads can properly support game-day traffic on business days during the afternoon rush, which, of course, is when most of the Marlins games will start. If I am proven wrong, so be it, but I certainly don't want to try it, personally.

Have you heard whether or not the Marlins will recognize any of the extensive history of Miami baseball or the history of the Orange Bowl in their new stadium? Do you think they should?

I think they absolutely should. There is obviously a tremendous amount of college and pro football history with the OB but there is also a bit of baseball history there. In 1956, the Miami Marlins played a game there in front of a sold out house and Satchel Paige was the Marlins starting pitcher. And the Caribbean League Championship Series was played there in 1990 and I attended one of those games. Also, Miami Stadium's predecessor, Miami Field, was located in the Southwest corner of the OB parking lot. That stadium was before my time but I had some relatives whom attended games there. I'm not sure to what extent they will honor all of that history, but, so far, I understand they are building some kind of artistic monument piece that is made from the Orange Bowl's main sign. So, while I think that is nice, it doesn't make up for the fact that an important and large piece of Miami sports history was destroyed unnecessarily, in my view.

What are your feelings on the Marlins becoming the Miami Marlins?

I have very mixed feelings about that and about them even being called the Marlins in the first place. On the one hand, it is nice as an honor to history, but on the other hand, it was a completely new team and completely separate from the two minor league franchises that used the name at Miami Stadium, so I always thought they should have a completely new name. And, of course, I fully understood that they used "Florida" in the name to appeal to fans all over the state and not just in Miami. So, I understand why many of the Marlins' fans in Broward, Palm Beach and other counties, are unhappy about the upcoming ˜change to Miami Marlins. I don't blame them. And to me, the Miami Marlins name will always refer to the team I grew up watching in the 80s and the eras prior to that. So, if it were up to me, I would give them a totally new name or would at least keep it as it stands currently, as the Florida Marlins. But, it is what it is. I will have to just get used to it.

What's next for your history projects?

I'm always interested in doing or contributing to any projects related to the history of pro baseball and Spring Training in Miami, as well as other parts of Florida. The Miracle has asked me to be involved in their celebration of that franchise's 20-year anniversary of moving to Fort Myers, so I am looking forward to that. Also, just today, in fact, a local historic preservation group contacted me about using some of my pictures and an article on their website. So, I am happy that there is still an interest out there.

You worked briefly in the front office of the Fort Myers Miracle. Why move with the franchise after it left Miami?

Initially, I wasn't at all happy that the franchise moved out of Miami, first to Hialeah, then to the West Miami area, on the campus of FIU and then to Pompano Beach for two years before finally settling in Fort Myers. I went to see them in each location and actually worked for them part time in Miami, Hialeah and FIU prior to Fort Myers, meeting some great people along the way, most notably Marlins GM Sonny Hirsch, who was a local Miami sports legend and worked in radio and TV and also in the Marlins/Orioles front office for about 30 years. I miss him and wish I could've worked for him much longer. But, after a while, I became more accepting and more comfortable with each of those moves because I understand all too well that, ultimately, the baseball business is just that—a business. They had to make those moves for business purposes and I can't blame them for that. They have found great business success in Fort Myers, under the leadership of Mike Veeck and Marv Goldklang. And after a while, it just came to the point that the Miami area was not the right environment to sustain minor league baseball. So, I am happy that they have found a suitable home over there on the west coast of Florida. There were very few regular fans left in the franchise's Miami fan base by the time the '80s came around. There were some great fans but just not enough of them. But, in Fort Myers, there are a lot of very passionate baseball fans over there who love minor league ball and give them the support that they just weren't able to get enough of during their last several years in the Miami area. Plus I enjoyed working and living in Fort Myers while I was with their front office. It would have been really nice for me to work full time in Miami Stadium, though, because it was my first love but I wouldn't trade my experience in Fort Myers for anything. I met a lot of great fans and worked with a lot of great people over there, as well, and I learned a lot from them, about the sports industry and about life.

Do you feel the Miracle have a responsibility to acknowledge the history of the franchise now that they are in Fort Myers?

Yes, I think every pro sports franchise owes that to their fans and to themselves. Tradition and history is such a huge part of sports, but particularly to pro baseball, in my opinion. Generally, the Miracle has been very open to honoring their franchise's rich and varied history. And I am always honored and happy to help them do that in whatever way I can.

--Originally posted October 10, 12, 14 by Mike Lortz

Greg Young
Modesto Nuts Broadcaster

Modesto is a long time member of the Cal League. For 30 years the franchise was known as the Modesto A's, but when Oakland switched Cal League affiliates to Stockton in 2005, Modesto affiliated with the Colorado Rockies and rebranded as the Nuts.

Greg Young has been working with the Nuts since 2007, and he's been their full-time play-by-play guy since 2008. On Tuesday, June 21st, Modesto hosted the California-Carolina League All-Star Game at John Thurman Field. I interviewed Greg several days prior about the game and his broadcasting career.

Aside from the All-Star game itself on Tuesday, June 21st, what are some of the other surrounding events fans can enjoy in Modesto?

Our front office is going with an "American Graffiti" style theme for all of the upcoming All-Star Game festivities. The event is being coined the "2011 All-Star Smash" and will kick off with the "Clutch Poppin' Parade" on Monday, June 20th. The "Clutch Poppin' Parade" will be a welcome reception featuring "graffiti" style cars and a short parade ending at the Gallo Center in downtown Modesto. The All-Stars will arrive to the Gallo Center gathering in "graffiti" style cars and will be introduced one-by-one to the crowd. The event will end with a Fan Fest where fans can interact and meet the All-Stars. It should be a lot of fun and a good way for Modesto to show off a little. Modesto's downtown area is very nice and it will be fun to see it on display for everyone coming out to see the events. We'll also have the home run derby before the game.

You haven't seen every team around the league yet, but who are some of the players you think fans could see in the All-Star game next month?

Once again San Jose is loaded with prospects and I'd imagine we will see several guys from that team at the All-Star Smash. Right now I would guess Gary Brown and Zack Wheeler from San Jose will be on hand. I've liked what I've seen from Matt Davidson and Bobby Borchering in Visalia and would not be surprised to see those guys there that week. It would be great to see Modesto's own Blake Smith make an appearance at the All-Star Smash. He's having a good season with Rancho Cucamonga and might have a chance to make the team. Eric Campbell of the Blaze is a stone cold lock to make the team, but that's assuming he's still in the league come All-Star time. I think there is a good chance we see a few Modesto players make it this year. Mike Zuanich, like Campbell, has to be on the Cal. League team this year. Zuanich is having a monster season and has become a huge fan favorite in Modesto. Both Dan Houston and Chad Bettis have put up All-Star numbers halfway through the first 70 games. It would be nice to see both of them make it, and maybe we'll see one of them start the game. We had three Nuts players on the 2010 Cal League team and there's a good chance we will see that happen again this season.

Broadcasting the game will surely be one of the higlights of your career. What are some of the other memorable moments in your career so far?

The 2011 All-Star Smash will certainly be a big highlight. Looking back I guess I would say I am most fond of my experiences in the 2010 playoffs. The Nuts swept the Ports in the first round last year with incredible performances from Rob Scahill and Juan Nicasio. Those two starters had outstanding seasons in 2010, and both put exclamation points on their years with those playoff starts. Modesto was eventually swept in the second round by San Jose, but making it that far was a lot of fun.

I was lucky to get my start as a play-by-play broadcaster with the California Cougars of the Major Indoor Soccer League back in 2006. I'll never forget my first road trip with that team and all of the great cities I was able to visit because of that job. The

Cougars moved to the Professional Arena Soccer League in 2008 and went on to win the league championship in March 2009. Despite how manufactured it felt, the experience of calling a championship run was still incredible. The Cougars had to win a tense overtime (golden goal, sudden death) semi-final match over the Edmonton Drillers to advance to the finals against Cincinnati that weekend.

That match was the most emotionally draining game I have ever been a part of. I wasn't a soccer fan entering that job, but I definitely grew to love that sport the longer I worked there.

Can you talk about your career so far? When did you decide you wanted to become a broadcaster, and how did you get to where you are today?

I first decided I wanted to pursue a career in sports broadcasting back in my freshman year at Sonoma State University in 2000. The Communications program was impacted at SSU, so I transferred to Sacramento State in the spring of 2003. I jumped on with the student run radio station at Sac State in 2004 and immediately got involved with anything I could get my hands on. I started calling softball, baseball, football and basketball games at KSSU and hosted a weekly talk show. I was pegged the station's Sports Director in 2005 and started building a play-by-play demo as soon as possible. I graduated in 2005, but stayed around for some baseball and softball games in 2006. I eventually put together a demo and started sending it out in 2007. I stumbled upon the California Cougars opening while submitting my baseball demo to various minor league teams in October 2007. The Cougars (based in Stockton) decided they would hire their first broadcaster with help from a Sports Broadcasting course offered by Sacramento State's continuing education department. I had actually taken the course once already (it was taught by KTXL Sports Anchor Mark Demsky) and had to enroll a second time in order to qualify for the Cougars job. I worked as a Part-Time News Production Assistant with Mr. Demsky at the time the class was offered and he helped me eventually land the job with the Cougars. That was my first professional gig in sports broadcasting and a few months later I was called to come down and do some work with the Nuts. I was actually hired to be Joshua Suchon's back up on AM 970's Modesto's Morning News program and was allowed to call home games with the Nuts as an added incentive. Suchon was the Nuts broadcaster in 2007 and I served essentially as an unpaid intern. I called three innings a night and worked all of the home games for free. Suchon left the Nuts in 2008 for a job with the Los Angeles Dodgers and I was hired by Modesto to take over for him.

What are some of the goals for the rest of your career?

Some of my old co-workers at KTXL advised me to shy away from goals, or more importantly time tables when it comes to my career. I just try and take it all one day at a time and just focus on whatever it is I'm currently working on. I guess it's nice to say my goal is to move up to the higher levels and perhaps above Modesto at some point. But, that is really easier said than done. It's very hard to move up in this business and you have to be very patient while waiting for a break. I just want to make the best of the situation I am in right now and put my best foot forward every day.

Growing up and even now, who are your favorite broadcasters, and even though everyone has their own style, is there anyone that you emulate a little when calling a game?

I grew up and still am a San Francisco Giants fan. The broadcast team of Jon Miller, Dave Flemming, Mike Krukow and Duane Kuiper is arguably the best in baseball. I love listening to all four of them call a game. I especially love the way Miller calls a game on the radio. I probably emulate (or steal) most of what I do from him. I think I've begun to develop my own style over my last two seasons in Modesto, but I still catch myself doing my best Miller impersonation every night.

The Bus Leagues Experience

I know that minor league front offices are small, and a lot of employees have multiple duties. Do you do anything else for Modesto besides the radio broadcasts, particularly in the offseason?

I'm actually only required to call the games and do some media relations type work with the Nuts. I write the daily game notes, collect line ups, deliver boxscores and write the daily game recap for the website. I guess I'm somewhat lucky that I don't have many other requirements outside of the games and those various media duties. However, my job is seasonal so my job begins and ends with the season opener and finale. In the past I was able to fill my off-season with the Indoor Soccer gig, but that is not an option anymore. I'm still looking for a way to fill that gap.

What is your favorite road trip in the Cal League and why?

I really enjoy going to Lake Elsinore. It's a long ride from Modesto to Lake E., but well worth it. The Diamond, in my opinion, is the best park in the league. The city may not be the best one to visit, but the park certainly makes the trip worth the long ride and stay. It also helps that Sean McCall (the voice of the Lake Elsinore Storm) is there every night with you in the press box. The Cal League is full of great broadcasters and great people. McCall is an incredibly entertaining broadcaster to listen to, and a truly great person to be around. Being able to visit with him and to visit that park is always a treat.

On the flipside, what is your least favorite and why?

Visalia is probably my least favorite trip. Bakersfield is a close second, but we do sit in an actual press box in Bakersfield. The visiting broadcaster sits outside in Visalia. Trust me it isn't a fun place to call a game.

You've been on the job since 2007. Who are some of the players that have stood out to you the most passing through the Cal League?

We had Dexter Fowler, Chris Nelson, Eric Young Jr., and Brandon Hynick during my first year in Modesto. We all knew Fowler was going to make it to the bigs at some point and it was fun getting a chance to work with him every night. Nelson, Young and Hynick had career years with the Nuts that season. Hynick was the Cal League pitcher of the year and went all of April without allowing an earned run. His starts were incredible that year and it was great seeing the league ace pitch every week. Watching EY Jr. steal bag after bag in 2007 is something that I'll hold on to for a while too. The Rockies sent us Jhoulys Chacin in 2008 and seeing him grow into a top of the rotation type starter in Colorado has been exciting. I also enjoyed working with Esmil Rogers and Aneury Rodriguez that season. Charlie Blackmon and Wilin Rosario were fun to watch play back in 2009 and 2010 featured Tim Wheeler from Sacramento State. I saw Wheeler's older brother during my time at Sac State and it was pretty cool seeing a fellow Hornet succeed in Modesto. I'm excited to see what Juan Nicasio, Rex Brothers, Rob Scahill and Adam Jorgenson do at the higher levels. I hope the best for all of those guys and everyone else that has come through Modesto. I'll be rooting for them every night that they aren't playing the World Champs.

--Originally posted May 21, 2011 by Scott Grauer

Players

The Bus Leagues Experience

Dellin Betances
Trenton Thunder (New York Yankees)

Dellin Betances is one of the Yankees' top prospects and one of the best in baseball. His career got off to a bit of a slow start, not reaching a full season league until his second full year of pro ball. In 2009, he had to have elbow surgery, further delaying his trip to the majors. In 2010, he came back as a dominant pitcher, and now he's at the Yankees' Double-A affiliate in Trenton. On Sunday, I talked with him before their game against Reading.

Thanks to my inability to make sure my recorder is working, half of this interview disappeared forever. I am 100% positive that the red light was on when we started, and for some reason it just went off. I'll still post what I have and hopefully next time I can post an entire interview. This will pick up after I asked him if the Yankees have talked to him lately about promotions later this season.

Well I mean honestly I haven't heard anything. I just been trying to go out there and pitch every five days wherever I'm at. I'm just trying to do the best I can.

Do you think there's any pressure or distraction pitching before the trading deadline since the Yankees are always pretty active?

No, I mean I've never had pressure. Honestly, I've really learned to not think about it much. If anything happens, then it happens. I just got to do my job which is pitch.

This was your first year in major league spring training. What was that experience like?

It was a great experience. It was an honor being able to wear the pinstripes with guys that I'm used to seeing and admiring on TV. Just to be around those guys it was definitely a surreal feeling.

You grew up a Yankees fan, right?

Yeah, I grew up a Yankees fan, so that made it a lot more meaningful.

When you were drafted, was it a hard decision to sign versus going to Vanderbilt?

It was a tough decision, but you know, when it came down to being picked by the Yankees, it made it easier. Obviously, I did a lot of things. I was able to move out and get my parents a house, so it was kind of nice to do that. I'm enjoying being here with this Yankees organization. They've treated me well, and I just hope that I can make the best out of it here or if not, elsewhere.

One of the questions analysts have about you is your durability, like your career high in innings pitched isn't very high. Do you think there's any potential that you end up as a closer down the road?

I pitched over 100 (innings) in 2008, and that's the only year. This year I'm probably going to pitch more than that, and that's one of my goals coming into this year, just trying to stay healthy and pitch as much as I can. As of right now, things have been going good, and I feel good now. It's just one of those things, as long as I'm in the majors, whether it's relieving or starting, I just want to contribute and help win championships.

How was your experience at the Eastern League All-Star Game last week?

It was a lot of fun. I was able to share that moment with a couple of my teammates: Manny (Banuelos), (catcher Austin) Romine and Corban Joseph. We all did fairly well, but it was a great experience. It was my first time making an All-Star Game and being healthy, and that was one of my goals coming in. I'm glad I was able to make it.

Betances went 4-6 with a 3.42 ERA for the Thunder before being promoted

81

to Scranton/Wilkes-Barre in late August. He was 0-3, 5.14 in four games there. He made his major league debut with the Yankees on September 22, walking four batters and hitting another in 2/3 of an inning.

--Originally posted July 21, 2011 by Scott Grauer

Tiffany Brooks
Arizona Summer League

Tiffany Brooks is the first American professional female baseball player to play in the Arizona Summer League, a professional instructional/ prospect league affiliated with the independent North American League. The league is based in Yuma, Arizona, and is made up of four teams and 57 players. Tiffany was drafted onto Team Canada, run by ex-MLB Pitcher Kip Gross.

Tiffany is no stranger to Arizona, having played in the Arizona Winter League in Yuma in 2010. On those January afternoons she often walked the mile back to her hotel room in the 85 degree heat and said she loved it here in winter, but there was no way she'd ever want to be here in the middle of summer. But fate has a funny way of getting back at baseball players, and now, here she is back in Yuma playing in the Arizona Summer League where just 10 days ago it was 120 degrees. When I came out to interview Tiffany (who is known as "Brooksie" to most of her teammates) a local said "it was a cool day" with temperatures reaching "only" 103 degrees, and on Sunday the temperature climbed to 110 degrees.

Tiffany is over six feet tall, and she's easy to spot on the field with her long, curly blonde hair pulled through the hole in the back of her ball cap. This past Saturday she had a day off from pitching and took on the duty of first base coach. It was obvious from the high fives from each of her teammates that passed her rounding first base the guys enjoyed having her out there and coaching them during the game against Long Beach Armada.

Immediately following Saturday's game Tiffany headed directly to the bullpen for instruction from her team manager and former MLB pitcher, Kip Gross. Kip is a straight forward type of guy. "Breathe out before you pitch" and "Don't make a step out of it…drive and glide down the hill" he told her. Tiffany took his instruction well and made immediate corrections.

Tell me about your first day in Spring Training.

Nick Belmonte runs Spring Training. He's a scout for the Red Sox, and he knows his stuff. He is a little like I'd imagine a drill sergeant might be. He's a great guy, and has connections all throughout baseball. Spring Training is two full days, and Nick runs a tight ship. I played in scrimmage and pitched two innings, striking out two, gave up one hit, and had a few other little things happen, but we won't talk about those [laughs].

In Spring Training which hitter did you think would be the toughest to face while pitching in the Arizona Summer League?

In Spring Training the pitchers and position players trained separately. Then we would come together for scrimmages. I watched this one guy [Stephen Tedesco] who was just hammering the ball. Someone said he was 11 for 11 at the plate in Spring Training or something ridiculous, so I kept a close eye on him. I wanted to face him to challenge myself but I didn't want to go out and have him take me yard either. As it turned out I got lucky – he ended up on my team, thank God!

Do you study players before pitching to them?

Absolutely! Yeah, I come out early sometimes or stay a bit for the later game and sit down and watch. Today I watched third baseman #9 (Bunya Maeda) on the Long Beach Armada team. He is a Japanese player and a good hitter, and now I know how I'll pitch him next time.

Do you find as a woman you have to work just a little bit harder than the guys to prove yourself, and is there one part of your game that you have worked on to help get you there?

As a prospect first baseman one reason I've not been as attractive to sign as I might be is that I don't hit enough homeruns. I have solid glove work and good footwork at first base, and I can hit for average and get doubles, but in baseball today, the corners are expected to be homerun hitters. If the wind is blowing out, the baseball gods love me that day, and someone grooves one for me, then I can go yard. Unfortunately all three of those things don't happen often enough for me! My other love has always been pitching, and I've done both that and play first base since Little League, so I began focusing more on my pitching in the last couple of years. I'm not typically a starting pitcher. I'm most effective as a one to two inning reliever either in the middle or sometimes as a closer, and can sometimes go longer if needed. When a manager knows how to use me – usually preceded and followed by guys with some heat – I can be pretty effective messing with hitters' timing, as I have a wide range of speeds and pitches I can throw, anywhere in a range of about 50-80 mph.

As a woman in baseball is it hard to find equipment or gear that fits your needs?

Oh yeah — Baseball pants never fit properly. Jerseys aren't cut for women, so I usually have to get a size that is way too big. If I play for a team long enough I consider getting the jersey tailored for my body. Many women's cleats are manufactured more for comfort and not as much for function as I'd like them to be. I usually wear men's spikes, but since women's feet are generally more narrow than men's I can't usually get a full leather cleat, as to cinch them down for a good fit. I need to get ones that are at least part fabric. If the ball cap doesn't have a hole in the back, I cut one out with scissors to pull my ponytail through.

Where are your sights set on playing next after the Arizona Summer League?

Well, like any of us out here, we have dreams of playing for a Major League team, and that means the first step is to be signed into affiliated ball. The truth of the matter is that I love the game so much, I'd play on the back side of the moon for a buck! Realistically, I'd love to play for the North American League, Yuma in particular. The Scorpions have a great organization with great players on that team, and I'd be really honored to join them or another team in the NAL.

What are your hopes for Brooks Baseball and Softball Academy?

In the future, I'd like to own several academies across different locations, but the next step for me is to buy an actual building. I have all the equipment I need to give lessons, and in summer and fall it's no problem to be outside, but I have to rent space in the early spring and certainly in winter.

What do you want people to know about you that hasn't already been covered?

I think it's really important for people to know that I feel extremely honored to be able to play this great game. Every time I button up my jersey, I know I'm very, very lucky, and that many people never get to go this far in the game. I would never be able to do it without people who love me and believe in me, without my generous sponsors, and without all the women and girls who e-mail me or come out to watch me play. I would also like people to know that while I may be the first female American professional baseball player in Arizona Summer League history, I surely won't be the last! There are currently two female baseball players headed to play in college this next year, and over 1,000 girls now playing at the high school level. I think you will see a lot more female ballplayers in the very near future, and I hope one day, in Major League Baseball. Play hard and dream big!

--Originally posted July 20, 2011 by Tamara Swindler

Chris Cates
New Britain Rock Cats (Minnesota Twins)

New Britain's Chris Cates is known for being one of the smallest players, physically, in Minor League Baseball. While waiting for batting practice to finish so I could talk to him last Wednesday, however, an exchange with a Rock Cats staffer told me how important he is to the team.

"So who are you looking to talk to?" he asked.

"Looking at Chris Cates," I said.

"Great guy," he said without hesitation. "He can play on my team any day."

Cates, as you'll see from his responses, is one of those interesting players who doesn't post great numbers — .210/.270/.246 in 52 games this season — but tries to help the team by doing the little things, and his positive attitude shows. He's the kind of guy you root for, even when you're not really supposed to be rooting for anybody.

We spoke for a few minutes about his daily routine, what roster turnover means to a team, and the most creative height-related comment he's ever received.

What's your daily routine like?

Get up. By then it's usually about 11:00 or so, so I'm trying to figure where I'm going to have lunch around 12:00, 'cause I don't like eating when I first get up, so I have to wait about an hour before I like to eat. So basically just get up, go to lunch, hang out in the hotel room until it's time for bus, and get here. We usually get here about an hour and a half before BP [batting practice], so you have time if you want to go get some swings in the cages, you just want to hang out and relax, just watch some TV, get something to eat, that sort of thing. I usually like to go hit in the cage, just get my swing ready for BP, and then after that get ready for BP, take BP, get the game, go home, do it all over again.

87

It's funny, I don't think I've ever heard it put like that – "get your swing ready for BP". Usually people think of BP as getting your swing ready for the game, but I've just never heard it phrased that way.

Yeah, I like to go in and do some drills, like some tee work. When we come out here for BP it's just live BP, so I like to do some tee work, maybe some short flips, or some soft toss, just kind of get my swing pattern going to where I want it to be so I can work on what I need to work on in BP.

At what point when you were younger did you realize that you may actually have a future in professional baseball?

You know, I was never really sure if I would get a chance to play pro ball. My older brother, he's a little bigger than me, he's about 5-foot-7, and I saw all the struggles he went through cause he was smaller and people not giving him the chance. When it was my turn to come around, I was a good five inches shorter than he was, so I thought it would be tough and it'd be a real challenge to play pro ball. But I knew that wasn't really in my hands, I really couldn't control it. All I could control was how hard I worked and how hard I played. I think it paid off because I knew I wasn't going to hit 30 homeruns, I wasn't going to hit .350 or better. I was going to be somebody who played good defense and did little things like put bunts down, try to get on base, hit and run, just little stuff that sometimes goes unnoticed. But that was my game and I knew that was the best way for me to have a chance to play at the next level.

You totally stole my next question, which was, "What are the things you do to help the team that don't show up in the box score," so thanks for that.

[laughs] Well, a lot of it too is when you're not playing as well you try to pick your teammates up, cause I'm one of the older guys on the team, I'm 26, and we've got a young team. I was here last

year, and just kind of trying to help them out as far as just knowing the game or knowing how the situations work. Just trying to give them advice to make them better players because you can't play every day like I'd like to but I figure what I try to do each day is what can I do to help the team win, whether it's if I'm playing or if I'm on the bench or coaching first or picking up pitches. Just trying to do something to help our team.

You guys had a tough year last year, in terms of wins and losses. This year it looks like you've bounced back a little bit, you're a little above .500, you're playing a little bit better. We always hear about minor league baseball being about player development, player development, player development, but how good does it feel to be winning some games now as compared to last year?

It feels a lot better, and I think a lot has to do with more experience, cause last year we had a young team and it was just one of those years where it seemed like no matter what we did we just couldn't win. Like if we had a lead late, we'd end up losing, or we'd go down early and we wouldn't come back. So one thing we did was just to forget about last year, cause every year is different. And we came out this year, we got off to a good start, and we're still playing well. We've had some guys go up and some guys get hurt so we've had new guys coming in, and in and out, just try to keep that momentum going. Cause we're only a few games back from second, from a playoff spot, so we're just trying to get a playoff spot and I think that would be a pretty good turnaround from what we had last year.

You talk about guys going up to Rochester. They've been struggling a lot, last year and also this year, and they've had a ton of roster turnover from what I've seen. From a player's viewpoint, how important is it to have a consistent roster?

I think it's very big because once you play with guys for a while, you start to know each other so well and know each other's weaknesses and strengths, and it makes a team more fun when you know people better and everybody's on the same page. We've had a lot of moves and we're still figuring out our team identity, whereas at the beginning of the year when we had the same team for a couple of months we knew what we were bringing to the table. I think it's really important that guys play together for a while because it takes a while to get used to playing with different teammates, but it's tough because it seems like once you get moving and more moves are made, new guys come in and you've got to start all over. So it's just a constant change to where you just got to throw what's dealt to you, I guess you could say. You just got to keep adjusting to the roster moves they make.

Now this may be looking ahead a little bit, but as far as when you're done as a player, what are you looking towards?

I want to coach. I've always had that, I guess you could say, "coaching feeling" in me, like in the offseason I like to do camps and lessons. I like working with younger kids and just passing on what I've learned. That's the way when I was growing up, anybody I could get information from, whether it be my brother or whoever was around, I'd try to pick their brains. So I have a desire to coach. I don't know exactly what level yet. I thought I wanted to do college, but I feel like maybe high school would be a little bit better for me because in high school I feel like you teach more. In college you kind of get there, you kind of know who the players are, and they're kind of defined as what they're going to be for the team. And then pro ball, obviously, you get to a point where you're pretty much established, you are who you are. I feel like I'd be better as a hands-on kind of coach. I could break down the game from the high school level and teach it – I don't know the correct way, I'm sure nobody knows the correct way – but teach it the way I've learned how to play from the coaches and players that I've been with.

Now, unless I'm mistaken, you have the longest current homerless streak in the minor leagues. I did the numbers a

**while back and it was close. Do you dream of hitting one
out someday, of just getting into one?**

Yeah, I've had a couple close calls. In 2008, we were playing in
Kane County, and I hit one off the wall. It's a double wall, so if it
hits the back wall it's a homerun, and I tried to plead with the
umpire that no no, it hit the back wall, and it did hit the bottom
wall. Last year I got into one at Reading that hit off the wall. But I
don't let it bother me. I know I'm not a homerun hitter. If it's
going to happen it's going to happen. I hit three in college and by
no means was I trying to hit 'em. I just got into a couple and one
was windblown. You know, I just try to hit the ball hard and put
it in play, and with me, I try to put the ball on the ground and
make the defense work a little bit, cause most of the time if I hit
something in the air it's not going to go very far so they're going
to have time to run it down. So I try to just hit hard line drives
and if I happen to get one up and it gets out, then absolutely I'll
be excited. That day may never come, but as long as I've got a
uniform and come out and contribute every day, that's pretty
much what I dream about.

**One of the things obviously that makes you a target for
opposing fans is your size. I heard it here a couple times last
night. Do you hear stuff like that at this point or are you just
tuning it out?**

[laughs] The thing is, a lot of people will say, "Did you hear that
ignorant fan?" or whatever, and personally, I have fun with it. It's
fun to me, as long as they're not yelling anything that's degrading
towards me, my family, my teammates. They're just out here
having fun, having a good time. We're out here to entertain the
fans. I mean, I've heard it all my life, so now it just comes to a
point where I try to see the best ones I can hear. I heard Oompa-
Loompa last night, and I've heard that one before.

**That was my next question, actually, was what's the most
creative – because you figure Oompa-Loompa, yeah, you**

probably get that all the time. It's like, "Step up your game, man, if you're going to mock me."

The best one I heard was actually in college. We were playing East Carolina, and somebody yelled out to mow the grass so the shortstop could see. That was probably the best one I've heard. But sometimes you get your fans who just yell, "Oh look, it's the SHORT-stop!" And I'm always like, "Come on, come up with something more original if you're going to chew on me or you're going to try to make fun of me." But like I said, I like to have fun with it, cause they're just out here having fun, cheering for their team, having a good time, so I don't usually let it bother me too much.

Cates spent the full season with New Britain, playing six different positions and hitting .205 in 79 games. He did not hit a homerun.

--Originally posted July 11, 2011 by Brian Moynahan

Travis d'Arnaud
New Hampshire Fisher Cats (Toronto Blue Jays)

One of three players* acquired from the Philadelphia Phillies in exchange for Roy Halladay in December 2009, Travis d'Arnaud is the top catching prospect in the Blue Jays system and the 36th ranked prospect on Baseball America's preseason Top 100. Currently playing for the New Hampshire Fisher Cats, d'Arnaud sat down with me before this evening's game against Portland to talk about what it's like being on the disabled list, how he and his brother (Pirates prospect Chase d'Arnaud) have helped each other deal with life in the minors, and what he does to earn the confidence of the pitchers on his staff.

*The other players Toronto received for Halladay were Kyle Drabek and Michael Taylor. Taylor was quickly flipped to the Athletics for Brett Wallace, who was then traded seven months later to Houston for Anthony Gose, who had just been acquired by the Astros from the Phillies, where he was a teammate of Travis d'Arnaud in 2009.

Must be good to be back playing now, after you missed a little time.

Yeah, I'm feeling really good now. After last year, only playing what, fifty games? That was a hard year for me, especially mentally, just not being able to be out there with the guys, playing every night. I just sat on the sidelines, just watching and started missing, missing playing a lot. I mean, already this year I had a concussion, so I was out a week and a half, and that same feeling was coming back, so yesterday I felt like it was Opening Day all over again. I just love playing, man. Like, I'm supposed to be at home right now but instead I chose to come here and do what I love, man, I love playing baseball. So, keep playing.

Kinda like a little kid on Christmas, you wake up...

Yeah, you wake up, going to open presents and stuff, it's just like me when the game starts.

93

The family connection is really one of my favorite things. Your brother Chase is in the Pirates system. Are you guys close?

Yeah, we're really close.

So during the season, are you talking a lot?

Yeah, we always text, talk, video chat, everything. We do all that stuff.

Is a lot of that about baseball or do you kind of get away from the baseball side? I know some guys I've talked to, they say when they talk to their siblings, it's like they don't even want to talk about baseball. It's more about catching up personally.

It's both. Seeing how his day's going, what he's been doing, how he's been playing. Just a little baseball but more off the field stuff, personal stuff.

You had at one point committed to play at Pepperdine with him. How close did that actually come to happening?

That was really close. I mean, if I didn't get drafted by the Phillies so high, I would've went without a doubt and played with him.

At what point did you guys realize that maybe you both had a shot at playing professionally?

I want to say…the start of my senior year, because he was drafted his senior year, not too high, so he went to school, and he had a feeling he would get drafted and I knew I was going to get drafted too, and at that time we were just like, we're both going to be playing, playing in the pros, maybe in the big leagues, hopefully on the same team one day. Cause we didn't get to at Pepperdine, so that's what we want to do.

Had you played on the same teams when you were younger? Like, when was the last time?

Only one year when he was 12 and I was 10, in Little League. That was the only time.

Not even in high school?

We went to different high schools.

There's a bunch of brothers and families in the minor leagues. There's three that come to mind right off the bat, and in all three of them, the younger brother is a catcher and the older brother is a middle infielder. Just based on your experience, is there any particular reason why that works out that way?

I don't know that there's a particular reason. I know he's way faster than me. He's way faster, more agile. I mean, I'm strong — we're both strong. When I was 12 I used to play shortstop. I guess from 12 to 18 I just didn't get any faster. So I just went behind the plate, started catching, and fell in love with it.

Obviously he's older, but you came right out of high school, so your professional career began earlier. Were you able to give him insight into what it was going to be like when he got drafted and signed?

Yeah, he kind of had an idea because he played in the Cape Cod Summer League, but I told him, it's a grind, it's really, really hard, cause you're gone from February until September and you can't go back home or anything, it's just baseball every day. I just told him to just always be happy, never look down on yourself, always think positive, stuff like that. That was pretty much all the advice I gave him.

The other side of that is that you're off to a little bit of a slow start this season, you mentioned you had the injury, and offensively it seemed like you were battling a little bit. He also got off to a slow start last year, in the same league, so have you guys talked about that at all, just the adjustment to Double-A?

Yeah, the adjustment? He just said, "Don't overthink anything. It's the same game as the first day you were playing when you were four years old until now. It's the same exact thing – it's a ball and a bat and you're throwing and swinging and try not to overthink it. Just play the game. Your instincts and your reactions are all going to come naturally. Same thing when you're hitting, too – if you overthink everything you're not going to be able to react in time to the ball, so just go up there and have the same approach you've always had. It's the same exact game."

Switching gears a little bit, on defense, one of my memories of watching baseball is, you see Jason Varitek, the catcher, the captain, sitting in the dugout, he's got a big three-ring binder in front of him, he's trying to figure out how to get an advantage on the hitters. Do you do that kind of prep work, first of all, and how much time do you spend on prepping for hitters?

I mean, I'm not Jason Varitek, he's one of the best catchers in the game right now, and I've never heard that three-ring binder thing, but for me, I just watch hitters, study them, even in the on-deck circle, I'll see how they set up, see what their swing looks like, and then before the game too with the manager and the pitching coach, we'll talk about each hitter and what their approach is, and at least what we think will get 'em out. But pretty much every day we talk about the lineup that we're facing.

Last season I talked to Kyle Drabek, and we talked a little bit about him coming over from the Phillies, and he referred to you as a "great catcher." What do you think that he and

the other pitchers on the staff see in you that makes them feel that way, that gives them that confidence in you?

I just get along with pitchers, really well. A lot of people say, "pitcher's personality." I don't know what that means, but every pitcher I've known I get along with really well. I understand how each pitcher's different, and I'm a really friendly person, I get along with everybody. And once I learn how they throw, then I can catch how they throw, how they like me to set up, where they want certain pitches, what they want in certain counts, so by the time the game comes it all just happens, so the flow of the game is better. They like throwing to me because I know what they want to throw in certain situations. And each pitcher too, when something bad happens they all react differently, so I need to know how to get them back to the right state of mind so they can keep pitching and forget about what just happened.

Your manager here is a guy who caught 11 seasons in the major leagues [Sal Fasano]. What have you learned from him just over the first few weeks?

I've learned a lot from him already in the first few weeks, a lot of it with game calling and situations. Like I said before, you know what the pitchers want to throw, but sometimes a certain pitch is needed for the certain situation, and I've talked to him a lot about that. And then a lot with how I receive the ball, too, like I've heard I'm a great receiver but I now I feel like I've gotten better, cause all the stuff he's taught me with blocking, with throwing, with game calling, like I said, just everything, he knows and understands it. Obviously, played 11 years, so for me it's just a huge learning experience because I can pick and choose what he tells me to apply to my game and so far it's helped me a lot.

So it's situational stuff but it's also your technique.

Yeah, technique, a lot of technique. Like receiving-wise, blocking technique so I'm more efficient blocking, just a lot quicker, receiving-wise, a lot more efficient. I'm able to stick the ball now instead of sometimes my glove would fall back but now it's just nice and firm and everything.

Last thing: the Blue Jays organization has some quality catching prospects, you know, you got [JP] Arencibia, Carlos Perez, Brian Jeroloman, just a few guys. A lot of stuff I've read says that you're considered, in the future, the guy who could hold down the starting catching job in the big leagues. Does it motivate you to look at those other guys that are coming up and say, "I got to work harder, I got to do more because it doesn't matter what people say now, these guys are coming and they want the same job that I do"?

Well, Carlos is a great catcher. I've seen him and he's going to be a great player one day, and me watching him, what he does, makes me want to work harder, like I want the same thing he wants, you know? So I need to work hard to make sure I can get there and stay there. He's doing the same thing, you know? I wouldn't necessarily say I look down on them – J.P., he's a great guy, ever since I came over here, him and [Travis] Snider have actually helped me and Kyle a lot, you know, learning everybody and getting to know everybody, and me just worrying about my game. I'm hoping for him and for Carlos, they both do great because they're both great guys, but for me I'm just working hard. Seeing what they do makes me want to work harder so I can be just as good or better than them.

After a slow start, d'Arnaud bounced back to hit .311 with 21 homeruns and 78 RBIs for the Eastern League champion Fisher Cats. For his troubles, he was named the league's Most Valuable Player. His brother Chase made his Major League debut on June 24 and appeared in 48 games with the Pittsburgh Pirates.

--Originally posted May 9, 2011 by Brian Moynahan

Wes Etheridge
New Hampshire Fisher Cats (Toronto Blue Jays)

I was at a playoff game in Manchester last week when I looked at the roster for the New Hampshire Fisher Cats. I didn't get to many games in the Queen City in August and had lost touch with what was going on with the team, so it was a surprise to see Wes Etheridge listed.

Etheridge was the Bus Leagues Independent Pitcher of the Year in 2010 after a season in which he went 10-0 with a 1.76 ERA for Na Koa Ikaika Maui in the Golden League. After pitching in Venezuela over the winter, he signed with the Blue Jays. As a closer with Dunedin this season, he saved 32 games with a 1.89 ERA.

His story is more interesting than your regular "Indy to Affiliated" tale. Earlier this season, I read a story on MiLB.com about Etheridge's journey over the past few years - specifically, his decision to quit baseball at one point and devote his life to becoming a pastor and studying the Bible.

We sat down for a few minutes before tonight's Eastern League Championship Series game to discuss that journey, what it was like to pitch in Hawaii, and what he expects from the future.

The Cliff Notes version, from my perspective, is that you played ball all up through college and everything, got drafted, and then decided that you needed to pursue something else.

Yeah, in a nutshell, that's basically what it was. And looking back now, how I view it now, I wasn't raised in the church. I didn't know anything about, basically, life. I just lived according to what I felt like doing, and then you get to a certain age and you start thinking, "What am I doing? Why am I here?" and all that kind of stuff. I found the Bible and then I never really got a chance to explore it because I was playing baseball, and I personally felt like that was my calling – to go study the Bible, be a pastor – and it really wasn't. That was my doing, I wanted to do it, and then I was kind of running into walls as I was trying to be a pastor, and I felt like God's like, "I gave you a talent, go use it! You're an idiot!" Kind of smacking me.

And sometimes that's what it takes, you know? And then I realized I loved baseball. Before, you don't know because it's all I've always done. My dad was all into it, pushed me into it, which I'm thankful for but I never really knew what else was in the world.

So you needed some time to figure out what was out there for you.

Yeah, you know, you get in your head, like, "I'm talented, I can do whatever I want." That's not exactly how I was thinking, but it's kind of a pompous attitude, like, "Oh, I can go be good in school, or go do this," when realistically, I can throw a sinking fastball. That's my talent, that's what God gave me. I'm not a basketball player, I'm not a musician, I'm not any of that. I'm a pitcher.

What was the thought process when you decided you were going to leave the game behind and go be a pastor? You kind of described it a little bit, but what was the process there?

It was a month, couple months, where I was just depressed. I would talk to my dad, and he knew it was coming, even though he didn't want to believe it. I just wasn't happy. I wasn't happy with myself, I wasn't happy with the way things were going, and I felt like I wasn't helping anybody, especially myself, by trying to do something I didn't want to do anymore. And it had nothing to do with the game or the way people treated me, the way the Brewers treated me. It was just mentally, I wasn't stable enough to handle it. My mind was elsewhere and I wanted to study the Bible, basically is what it came down to.

Is that something you're still involved in now that you've come back to baseball?

Yeah, I mean, it's almost like the ace in my pocket. God IS a crutch. I don't care, people make fun of me – or not make fun of me, but make fun of people like, "Oh, God's your crutch" – yeah, it is. I know where to go when I'm having problems. I go to the Bible, but it's not the same. I'm a baseball player that believes Jesus Christ died and rose from the dead. I'm not a pastor, I'm not a deacon in the church, anything like that. I'm a baseball player and those are my beliefs. I'm not a preacher, I'm not on the corner preaching it, but personally it's something that will never leave me.

So is being a pastor, I guess you could say "witnessing", is that something that you could see yourself going back to and making another attempt at after baseball's done?

I can see it happening. Whether or not it will I don't know. That's something just like, we don't know where we're going to be tomorrow, me and you, so it's kind of one of those things like the more I think about something like that the more you're just kicking the wind. You're really not doing much. But yeah, in a perfect world I'd love to play baseball until I'm 40, retire, and be a youth pastor and help the kids in my neighborhood. That'd be a great life, but I don't know what the plans are.

When you decided to get back into baseball, what was the process like there?

The process was, I got a phone call from a guy – this story's been told, you probably heard this – and he said, "God doesn't need you to be a pastor. I think you should go play baseball." That's the short story. And then I called the Brewers, because I'd been away from them for 18 months. I was like, "Look, I'm thinking about going to play. I understand I left you guys. I just wanted to let you know if you want me, I owe it to you guys to come back, but if not I'm going to continue and try to play." They said,

"We'll call you back." They called me back in a few weeks, and this is January bordering February at the time, and they're like, "Yeah, come to spring training."

I'm in no way ready to play. But I go back and pitched good, and then they released me last day of spring training. Steve Springer, who's with the Blue Jays, I called him immediately, I'm like wow, this isn't...you think God sends you to do something and you're all excited, and all of a sudden you don't have a job. I called him kind of like, don't know what to do, he's like, "Let me make a phone call." Calls Cory Snyder in Maui, he sets me up for a tryout. Their spring trainings in indy ball, you're not guaranteed anything. So I went out there and threw well out there, and was in the coolest place in the United States, personally that's what I feel. The team disbanded I think this year, so they really had one season, and I got to play in Maui for the only season it had a baseball team. So when you look at it like that, God's hand was definitely in it.

What's that like, playing baseball there? It's not someplace you normally think of as a baseball hotbed.

It's unbelievable. It might not be a baseball hotbed, but the players that do play in Hawaii are unbelievably talented. I think their biggest problem is they don't want to leave the island. It's just a different world, beautiful, it's unbelievable. And I surf, so it was perfect for me. I'd get that little homesickness, I'd go surf and I'd be fine. It was a good transition from playing with the Brewers, not liking it, but it was kind of like I had a year where it was in-between real – it's not like real life in Hawaii. You can go play baseball and go to the beach. It kind of was like a buffer for this year for me. This is like real baseball.

Do you think that being there – you said you had surfing, you were able to relax a little bit – do you think that contributed to the year you had last year?

I think it did 100% because baseball is a lot mental. I wouldn't put a percentage on it because I don't know, but most of it's mental, and when you're mentally locked in and that's where you want to be, and you're wearing board shorts to the field every day and I'm comfortable, I think it had a lot to do with the way I pitched. And then it was a good transition and then I got some confidence, like, "Maybe I CAN do this," and then I got a job in Venezuela. Threw well enough there – and I went there thinking, "I'm going to get lit up, I don't even know how they gave me a job" – pitched well there and then you start to believe, maybe God was right. Maybe I am a pitcher. Just kind of baby steps for me, because I wasn't ready. Last year was a good transition period for me.

And then all of a sudden this year you go down to Dunedin and you're one of the best closers in the minor leagues.

They put me in a role that they felt fit the way I pitched, and I just said, "Okay, we'll see what happens," and obviously it worked out. And I don't know what tomorrow holds or anything, but it's been a fun ride looking back now that I can reflect, it's been a good couple years.

Is that a role that you feel like you thrive in? Does it matter to you where you pitch?

No. In high school – and this is my dad, I'll knock my dad on this – he'd be like, "You're a starter because your first inning's always your worst." And I always thought starting was my thing, but now that I've pitched in every single role I could imagine, I realize it doesn't matter. As long as you're not mental with it, once you get on the mound you throw one pitch at a time. It's no different.

What's your repertoire like? You said you throw a sinking fastball...what else?

Basically, sinker is my pitch. If that's not working I'm not going to be effective. I complement it with a slider that's not devastating, but it works because they're sitting sinker. So basically sinker, slider, and a very occasional changeup.

So you try to keep guys off-balance?

I want to say I rely strictly on movement. Strictly on straight-down movement where I want early contact ground balls. I want four ground balls to every fly ball. That's my goal, and if I strike guys out, good, but that's not what I'm looking to do. I just want them to put the ball on the ground, and the higher I go the more I realize the defense is better, so it benefits me, the higher level, if I can still keep getting ground balls. You watch baseball, the infield here is unbelievable. You see Web Gems every day.

It sounds like you live in the moment. You don't really know what's coming tomorrow so you don't worry too much about it. But what's coming for you after the season?

Going to Venezuela again. I enjoyed that.

Is that something the Blue Jays suggested?

No, it's kind of weird how that happened. Our centerfielder in Maui last year has an agent that gets him winter ball jobs, an overseas agent, and he recommended me to him. The guy got me the job, he's a Puerto Rican guy and for whatever reason we hit it off and he's my real agent now. He's got good connections in Latin America, and even in Japan, so he got me the winter ball job.

Hopefully I can keep going back to the same team. I enjoyed it. Julio Franco's their coach, he's a born-again Christian too so I think he had a soft spot for me. It's kind of like it started last year, it's cutthroat over there: if you pitch well, you stay, if not, you go home. But I'd love to keep continuing that too.

After compiling a 1.89 ERA and 32 saves in 46 games with Dunedin, Etheridge finished the season in New Hampshire, posting a 3.94 ERA in eight games.

--Originally posted September 13, 2011 by Brian Moynahan

Anthony Gose

New Hampshire Fisher Cats (Toronto Blue Jays)

Early in the season, I sat down with New Hampshire Fisher Cats outfielder Anthony Gose prior to a game against the New Britain Rock Cats. We spoke about how a native Californian handles the New England weather, how it feels to be one of the youngest players in the Eastern League, and the benefits of having a former major league catcher as your manager. I did not ask him if he's ever heard, "There's two o's in Goose," but it's a long season.

It must've been killing you, some of the weather we were having [it had been in the 40s the previous week].

I don't mind, I've played in weather like this. So it's not too big of a deal as far as ever playing in weather like this. Obviously it's still cold and it's still a bit of a shock when you get here because coming from the Florida State League all season, being in warm weather, Florida, California, your body gets used to that again, and then you come up here and you get stung by the cold. I mean, it's a little bit different but hey, the season's got to go on.

So you still live in California?

No, I live in Florida now. I split time, really, between Florida and California, so I'm always in good weather, all year, for the most part, and now I'm here. But I heard it gets real nice in the summer time.

It does, it gets warm. Today was a nice sort of indicator of it. It's been beautiful all day.

Yeah, it's not as scary because now you go from freezing cold to now it's warm, so I'm kind of like, probably going to rain here pretty soon, one of these next few days. *[Ed. Note: it rained the next day.]*

106

Some days it goes quick. Yesterday it could be 30 degrees and then tomorrow it's 90. So you never know. Welcome to New England.

[laughs] It's different.

It's good prep for Canada.

That's the ultimate goal.

That's the dream to get up there, right?

Yeah, I mean, that's the whole goal.

It's not so cold up there when you're playing in the major leagues.

No, I'm sure it's not. [laughs]

One of the things I wanted to ask you about is your defense. I was actually at the game last week, I think it was last Thursday, ninth inning, tie ballgame, there was a guy on, and you went into the gap – it was a slicing line drive – you went into the gap and you laid out for it. Tracked it down. And the first thing I thought of was, I had to wonder what's going through your head when you see a ball like that go up, and you know you're going to have a long way to go. What's running through your mind? IS there anything running through your mind or is it just that your instincts take over?

God, I have to say instincts probably. Not too much thought that goes into it, really. I mean, I don't know what other guys do or how they think, but before the pitch is coming I'm thinking I'm not going to let anything fall here. Then it's just a matter of getting to the ball, really, and making the catch. I don't really think about, you know, am I going to lay out here. Just kind of like you said, instinct and react to what's going on.

Do you ever get to a point where you think you can get to it and then you realize, you're almost there, and you go, "I'm not going to make it"?

There are certain cases. I'm not going to sit here and say I don't, because there's always times that things like that'll happen, where I think I've got a good bead on a ball and then all of a sudden it'll be a little bit farther than I had predetermined. That happens to everybody, I think, from infield to outfield, but it's definitely happened to me.

So you just play it as it is and go get the next one?

Yeah, once that happens, once it's already past me, there's nothing I can do but hurry up and get it in, to the cutoff man or the next infielder. Once it's by me, and there's no catch, it's time to do something different and get the ball in as fast as I can so we can stop the runner.

Now offensively, you're off to a slow start this year, in the first three weeks or so [he was hitting .185 as of the day we spoke]. How do you keep your confidence up when you're scuffling a little bit?

You know, the reason I have so much confidence right now is because I've never been at this point in my career to where I'm seeing the ball so good and not being able to get hits. I mean, everything…I've never felt this good in the box, honestly. I'm not swinging at balls in the dirt – obviously I do every once in a while, it happens – but for the most part I'm laying off breaking balls and changeups that have always been my biggest, I guess you could say, Kryptonite. Right now, at this point, what I'm doing and what I'm feeling up there is something I've never felt, so it's just a matter of, [the hits] are going to come. I'm going to get my hits, I'm going to hit, so I don't really worry. Confidence has never been an issue with me. I'm always real confident, and I like I said, I've never felt this good, and seeing the ball this good, and not gotten hits. So it's just like, got to keep going, rolling with the punches.

And you're one of the youngest guys, not only on the team, but you're one of the youngest guys in the whole league. What do you think of that?

It makes me feel good. Because like our manager [Sal Fasano] said a couple days ago, he gave us a talk and he said, "Who's to say you can't be 18 [years old] in the big leagues? Who's to say you can't be 17 in the big leagues?" Obviously it's very rare, but why can't I be 20 in the big leagues? And why can't I be the youngest here? It doesn't bother me. It makes me feel better. It makes me want to play better, show the older guys that a young guy like me can play the game with them. Because obviously, we have veterans on this team, especially the pitching staff. My thing is, I want the pitching staff to WANT me out there. I want everybody to want me on the field because they know I'm going to make the play, they know I'm going to make something happen. And that's the way I feel about it. It's kind of almost gaining their respect, in some sense, and getting everybody to notice that just because I'm young, I can play the game with anybody. That I'm ready.

Your first year in pro ball, you had a pretty good success rate on your stolen base attempts, I think it was around 80%. Last year was down to about 58% or so. Were you able to look at what you did last year and say, "This is why I struggled with that"?

Oh yeah, I mean, that instance came up all season long. Throughout the season, when I got caught, I just looked back and I said, "This is why I got caught. This is the reason why it happened. This is what I did wrong to get caught stealing that base." And the same sense went when I did something right, I'd say, if I stole a base easy, sometimes I'd look and I'd go, "Man, I haven't stolen a base that easy, that felt really good. I got to keep doing that." Now it's just a matter of being more consistent with it. But that was from every stolen base. I mean, that goes from when I'm in the box on offense to out there on defense, every time I go, "That felt good. I got to keep doing that." And then it's just a matter of getting my body to do that over and over and over, consistently.

So that consistency is what you're looking for?

That consistency, everywhere, no matter what part of the game, no matter what facet of the game, I've got to be consistent. That's what they do at the big league level. You know, [Jose] Bautista's the most consistent player in the big leagues right now, with his swing. And then there's outfielders who are the most consistent – you know, Torii Hunter, and Rajai *Davis [Ed. Note: Davis finished a rehab stint in New Hampshire last Wednesday]*, they're in the big leagues because they do everything consistently. And that's just where I've got to get myself at and get my body to do. Just do it over and over.

Who did you look up to as a kid, and then is there anybody that you model yourself after as a player?

When I was a kid…I liked baseball, I didn't really watch much, but one guy I did know because his name was always brought up around me was Juan Pierre, and I just kind of took him on as my favorite player. And then as I got older, started watching the game a little bit more and getting more in tune with it, I became a real big fan of Carl Crawford, watching him play, watching him on the highlights, seeing what he's doing, how he goes about the game. And I've kind of taken that in, as growing up was Juan Pierre and now has become Carl Crawford.

That's the guy you look at that you say, "If I could be him, that would be…"?

That'd be the guy.

I know that when you get on you like to run. I think I counted Opening Night it was like eight times or something you took off on a steal. Your manager here is Sal Fasano, former big league catcher. Does that have any effect on your learning curve as far as situations to run in, things to look for with the pitcher, the catcher, what the defense is thinking, stuff like that?

Oh, most definitely. Sal's great. Sal wants to always make the odds in my favor. Not just my favor, but any base runner on his team, he wants the odds in our favor. Sal's really big on situations, counts, the times – Sal's so good with numbers, he just adds the numbers so well and gives you exactly what's going on between the pitcher and the catcher, the pitcher to home plate, and the catcher to second base, that he lets you know right then if you can run or not. Then it's a matter of him knowing the game so well and catching in the big leagues for, I think it was about 13 years? Twelve, 13 years? He caught in the big leagues, caught the greatest guys, and being behind the plate, he knows the situations, and the counts, what time in the game, when's a good time to go, when's a good time not to go. You know, all that plays in such a big effect, and it's been great.

So he'll actually kind of show you and tell you the right way?

Yeah, I mean, he gives me the situation and the count. And you know who has been the biggest help, as far as technique, has been Justin Mashore, our hitting coach. He's given me so much, so much, not only offensively, but also on the base paths and in the outfield – he was said to be an unbelievable outfielder, you know, could run really fast and stole a lot of bases – he worked with me on the base paths and it's been unbelievable, the transformation from the things that he's taught me to when I just came in. I came in just doing it on ability and now he's given me a skill and a craft, almost, I guess you could say. I appreciate him so much because of what he has shown me and done for me and helped me out, out there and offensively. It's just been unbelievable.

111

Last July, I guess it was the 29th, you got traded to Houston for Roy Oswalt, which is kind of a cool thing in itself, and then almost right away you got traded over here to Toronto. What was going through your head that day? Were you hearing things that you might be dealt, and how quickly did it happen that you went from A to B to C?

You know, it didn't faze me, it didn't bother me one bit at all, honestly. I kind of expected to be traded, at the beginning of the season, just from other things that were going on, so I had already prepared myself, and I just was, if I'm going to get traded or if I want to get traded, I got to go out there and I got to play the game and do things right. So it wasn't really a big effect, you know, like they say, they always tell you about trades: it's a business also, which a lot of people look past but it is a business. And the big league team is where it's at, they want that team to win a World Series, so they're going to sacrifice some of the guys in the minor leagues to make the big league team better. So you can't ever think that you're not going to get traded or look past anything in any aspect like that of the game. You almost have to...I don't want to say "expect it", but you got to be ready for anything that can happen here.

And one of the other guys that writes for our site pointed out that you went from the Phillies team in the Florida State League to the Blue Jays team in the Florida State League. Did you notice anything with the fans or anything?

They're so close, you don't really notice too much of a difference. The parks, they got to be five minutes away from each other? I mean, it's literally across the street from each other. So you don't notice really too much of a difference in fans or anything like that. You're playing against them all season so those fans have been rooting against you, and now they're cheering for you, it's not really a big deal.

What are your goals for the rest of the year?

You know, the rest of the year…maybe be in Toronto. But really, honestly, just have a good season, help the team win. I've won a championship in Lakewood, helped win a championship in Lakewood, and that's an unbelievable feeling, to win a championship, to be a part of a winning team. That's the whole goal is to help the team win, finish strong, lead the team in as many ways and as best I can, and keep us rolling.

Gose hit .253 with 16 homeruns, 59 RBIs, and 70 stolen bases in 137 games for New Hampshire. At the end of the season into the playoffs, he stole 22 consecutive bases without being caught. I never told him there are two o's in goose.

--Originally posted May 3, 2011 by Brian Moynahan

Mark Hendrickson
Norfolk Tides (Baltimore Orioles)

A veteran of nine major league seasons, Mark Hendrickson failed to make the major league roster for the Baltimore Orioles out of Spring Training. He has appeared in twelve games for the organization's Triple-A affiliate in Norfolk, compiling an 0-3 record and 3.51 ERA in 33.1 innings as the long man in the Tides bullpen. After giving up nine earned runs in his first eight innings, he has settled in and allowed just four earned in his last 25.1.

I had a chance to sit down with Mark after batting practice last Friday at Syracuse's Alliance Bank Ballpark (and I owe him a special thanks, as I was late getting into town and missed our scheduled time). We talked about his background as a two-sport athlete, the importance of adjusting throughout the course of a career, and the mental challenge of returning to Triple-A after several years in the major leagues.

I was wondering if maybe first you could just talk to me about how your time was budgeted between baseball and basketball growing up?

I grew up in Mount Vernon, Washington, which is kind of like the northeast when it comes to weather, for baseball. We played a lot in the summers because the weather wouldn't really allow us to get a whole lot of baseball in the spring, so I played basketball in the winter, baseball in the summer, and just kept doing it.

What people don't realize, I was fortunate to be on some very good teams in high school. Had a lot of success, both in basketball and in baseball, and I just wanted to go to college, and to me, college basketball was exciting, it was something I wanted to be a part of. I ended up signing at Washington State, and I always knew baseball was a summer sport, always knew I could play in the summers, and my biggest thing was that I had a lot of family around me that helped me make a good decision. When the draft came, out of high school, I wasn't ready to sign. I know that the scout I dealt with at the time, I kind of had a little bit of a sour taste, cause he probably tried to bully me into signing. But my grandfather had nothing to do with it, and my biggest thing was just wanting to control my rights. And once I signed on the dotted line I knew that if this team wants me to go to winter ball, if this team wants me to go to Spring Training, regardless of what the contract states, there was always a fear that that could happen, and then I wouldn't have control of what I wanted to do, and that was go to school, play college basketball.

That's how it started. Everybody thinks I had basketball more than baseball at the time, it was like, no, that was what I kind of wanted to do in college. So, that's how that got started, and I just kept playing baseball every summer. I had a unique situation where I got drafted every year, just because I never signed a letter of intent to play baseball, so I kept going back in the draft. It became a little comical, cause it wasn't like there was a whole lot of interest, other than getting drafted. There wasn't a lot of discussion, there wasn't a lot of negotiation. It was just a matter of a team picking me up, "Hey, if he wants to come play baseball, we'll do it." The Atlanta Braves, they're the team that got me out of high school, and they got me again down the road, and actually their scouting director came to my house cause my grandfather had him in school. So that was probably the closest I came to signing, but it just still wasn't the right time for me.

It finally came to fruition, and basketball progressed, and the NBA was there, and I put forth the effort to see what I could do there – all the while still playing baseball – and after my first year in the NBA Toronto picked me up in the draft. Followed me the whole summer – I was playing in some men's leagues down in Pennsylvania cause that's where my family's from – and I went out in September, went up to Toronto, worked out for them, and then the following spring I signed. We agreed to a contract to play in the summer, so I did that for three years, and then basketball was kind of one foot in, one foot out, wasn't really landing. After playing for parts of four years, just kind of said, "I wonder how good I can be in baseball?" So I committed full-time in the winter of 2000, and went to Spring Training, kind of got my feet wet, came here, Syracuse, played one full year here, and then the next year I played half a year and got called up.

So it was a situation where you decided that basketball had run its course.

Yeah, I mean, I played against some NBA guys that just...I would probably say my college coach put it best, he said I do a lot of things good but nothing great. And you get to the NBA level, it's a different style of game, guys are more athletic. I did okay, but I think the lure of pitching, being left-handed, having some advantages before I even step on the field, was intriguing to me, and I had only played a couple months a year, my whole life, after high school. So the lure of getting in shape, pitching, seeing how good I could be, was appealing. And I just remember that day I decided to go for it and say, "Hey, let's go." Because ironically it came after the fall league, which after my third year with Toronto they said, "Hey, we want you to go to the fall league," and I pretty much couldn't turn it down. My agent said, "If you want a future in baseball, you need to go."

I went, I was in the top 10 in ERA out there, had a very good fall league. Didn't get put on the 40-man – cause that was my third year, that was my protection year – I didn't get Rule 5, and that to me was just a sign that I need to commit more than three months to baseball. So that's kind of how that led to the full-time baseball in 2000.

One of the things that you notice a little bit with some of the taller guys, like a Randy Johnson or Andrew Brackman, it seems like they blossom a little bit later. Johnson was a little bit older when he really came on and Brackman's in his mid-20s and starting to pick it up. I know it's a little bit different for you because, like you said, you didn't really devote yourself to it when you were younger, but did you notice that things came to you differently than it seemed like they came to other guys, developmentally?

Yeah, pitching's a craft, no doubt. I mean, there's guys that throw the ball well, that have questionable athletic ability. There's guys who have great athletic ability, you put 'em on a mound and they're clueless. It's its own unique craft, and for me, I just have been blessed with athletic ability. I've been blessed with the ability to pick things up quickly. I swear to this day I made it to Double-A on strictly athletic ability. It wasn't anything more than just knowing how to compete and knowing my body.

Did you realize that at the time, that you were just kind of going on that?

Yeah, if you think about it, I was pitching in Double-A and I pitched two, three months a year, you know? It's not like I was dedicating any time in the offseason. I'd play catch to get my arm in shape and that was it. So, for most guys, they get to Double-A and not really put in the time, that's saying something. But it's just one of those things that that was probably one thing that I was blessed with, was just picking up things rather quickly. Even my growth spurt in high school, I didn't have any physical problems. I played point guard until I was a sophomore in high school and then I grew six inches in a summer and all of a sudden now I'm playing down low, doing a little bit of everything, but I just never really had any issues that you see with some taller guys.

So your game had to change entirely.

I just adapted. And that's touch. I think it goes with – it's amazing to me how you find some pitchers who can't play catch, who can't lob it. They don't have touch. I think a lot of the sports, because I played so many sports, I was able to take something from another sport and apply it. My touch – what I would say is I'm kind of a "touch and feel" guy on the pitching – obviously, I don't throw 95 – but my touch and feel has a lot to do with basketball. You know, playing around the hoop, having some touch, you got to have a little bit of finesse in your game, and I think that carries over to pitching.

117

So you don't have to be all power all the time. You CAN'T be all power all the time.

No, and most guys aren't. I mean, the guys that ARE power usually have no clue where it's going. Yes, you see the elite power guys up there, but that's the select few. What about the other guys that don't make it? They can't command it, and can't throw to a base. I think that, for me, I'm a firm believer of telling kids, "Hey, multiple sports." It keeps your interest. It does have attributes in both, in a lot of sports, that carry over, and you just don't get burned out. A lot of people try to pick a sport at such a young age, and then kids get burned out.

You mentioned adapting. As far as what you came up with for pitches, what you were throwing, how has that changed, or has it changed, over time, with what you're throwing now?

It changes over time. When I first came through this league 10 years ago, I learned how to pitch inside. I pitched inside, all of a sudden, I skyrocketed through Triple-A, and it was because of learning that the hitters down here are still developing. And so a lot of guys have a hard time hitting inside pitches. They have a hard time keeping inside pitches fair. They have a hard time with offspeed pitches. That's kind of the learning curve they're going through. I go up to the big leagues, that's how I start, and all of a sudden I get a reputation of, "Oh, he can pitch inside, he can pitch inside." Well, that was just a carryover from down here. But you play in the big leagues long enough, you have to start to adapt. You have to kind of start to see that guys in the big leagues can put it over the fence if you keep throwing inside, so you got to pick and choose, you got to work on different things.

And that's just the constant battle with professional sports, because you see the same guys, they've seen you, it's a cat-and-mouse game, and you got to adapt. If you don't adapt...very few pitchers or hitters have gone through their career not having to adapt. That's just the way the game is, and the guys that do, have a long career.

What's the difference between when you were playing in the minor leagues back then and now, when you're here this year?

This one is all mental. When I first came back, I got the news, I was very disappointed. [pause] First couple outings, I just didn't have anything mentally. I didn't know... [pause] I didn't even know if I wanted to pitch again. Because I just felt like I was a major league pitcher, I am a major league pitcher, that wasn't the case, I'm here in Triple-A. Mentally, to be up there for nine years and come back — I mean, I'm 10, 12, 14 years older than a lot of these guys. I told my wife, I said, "I just don't know." And I had to work through some of the emotions that came with not making the team, and just deal with all that comes with that. And if anything, that's the lesson I'm trying to teach these young guys. This league is all from the neck up. There are some physical skills that guys have to work on, but it's the constant dealing of different situations that are thrown at you. Whether it's your buddy getting called up, whether it's the road trips, the travel, there's a lot of things that, if you have some big league time, it's a tough road. If you're a young guy, it's a little bit different, it's kind of the next level. It's kind of like you don't know what you're missing, because you haven't been there. But for guys like us, which I think is some of our struggle, is we have a lot of guys who have a little bit of time. And it's tough. You got that taste, you got the emotions that come with being at Triple-A, not being in the big leagues. It's the biggest challenge of my career by far.

When the time comes to hang it up — you said you weren't really sure you wanted to pitch anymore at one point — do you think that your basketball career, having played basketball professionally and then leaving that behind, do you think that prepared you at all for when baseball ends? Or is it just entirely different?

119

Entirely different, cause I'm an athlete. I looove everything about being an athlete. I take care of myself, I eat well. I've been doing it since I was in high school. My college coach's wife remembers how I used to eat well in the airport. It's just something that I just have always loved to do. I have aspirations to play golf when I'm done. And not just recreationally. That lure is how good I can be at that sport, competitively. So I have that.

I think for me the biggest thing, too, to kind of make clear is: after the first couple outings down here, having gone through the process of the emotions I had, I've been able to refocus, to say, "Hey, this is just a challenge to get back," and when I get back I'm going to have learned a few things down here that's really going to pay off. So that's kind of where I'm at now. But very easily I could've gone the other way.

I think you see some guys, from watching on the outside looking in, I see guys that kind of go that way. They run into something...

And it can happen [snaps fingers] within a week. You can be great one week, the next week it can be all bent out of shape. And so, that's a challenge. For me it was always 40. I was always going to play until I was 40 and then just kind of see where I was at. Jamie Moyer's a great role model, just because I love the fact that he's adapted, adjusted, he's been around, he still loves playing, and that's kind of what I aspire to be. I want to play into my 40s and temporarily this is a little bit of a situation I just have to go through, which I'm fine with, and I'll get myself back. And we'll keep playing and we'll see what happens. You know, the family too, that kind of weighs on it.

After that, yeah, the transition. I don't know if anybody's ever really used to it. My wife and my family, we've committed our lives to it. When it's over, I think it's an adjustment for a lot of guys. Unless they're just completely burned out, but I've yet to find a place where I can find that adrenaline, that emotion that goes with being on a baseball field, or being on a basketball court prior to the game. Those are hard to find, that adrenaline rush and that feeling of butterflies in the stomach. I still get it. That's why I know the desire's still there. I still have it. So we will see. I'm sure I'll transition, but that time hasn't come quite yet.

Hendrickson returned to the big leagues with the Baltimore Orioles on July 9. He appeared in eight games, winning one and compiling a 5.73 ERA. In 24 games out of the bullpen in Norfolk, he was 2-4 with a 2.87 ERA.

--Originally posted May 26, 2011 by Brian Moynahan

Liam Hendriks
New Britain Rock Cats (Minnesota Twins)

A native of Perth, Australia, Liam Hendriks is the sixth-rated prospect in the Minnesota Twins system according to the Baseball America Prospect Handbook. I caught up with him after a game last week when his New Britain Rock Cats visited New Hampshire, and he answered a few questions about his health, the honor of representing his country in international competition, and the reasons for his professional success.

When I was looking for guys on the Rock Cats that might be interesting, I noticed in the Prospect Handbook for Baseball America that you used to play Australian Rules Football.

Yes, that is correct. I grew up playing that through my dad, he was pretty good at it back in the day, and then I grew up playing it and had to choose between baseball and football at one point.

When did you start playing baseball?

I started playing baseball — I obviously started in tee-ball when I was about five or six — and then I think my first year of baseball was when I was 12.

When did you kind of realize that this was something that you could go on forward with?

Maybe, like, I was about 15 or 16, where I had a couple of good years. I used to be a hitter, so I had a couple good years swinging the bat a little bit, and it just kept getting better and better, and I got invited down to the MLBAAP [Major League Baseball Australian Academy Program] program in Australia, where it's about the top 80 kids in Australia go down to this one place and they hang out and they train there for two months. So I got invited to that and I thought that's when I thought it might be a viable option for me to continue working in this and maybe it'll work out for me.

You've had some injuries that you've dealt with, I think they said a knee surgery and a back surgery. Was that related to football?

Not really. I've had two knee operations, both on the same knee, both doing the exact same thing. I did my first one sliding into second base, when I was hitting, and I did the next one on the mound. And that's pretty much the reason I decided to quit football and start following baseball a lot more because of the whole contact sport and stuff like that. And then the baseball thing was just a bit of a nerve injury that the nerve flared up in the base of my neck and started running through my ulnar nerve in my elbow.

Sounds like fun.

No, it was not fun at all, I started to lose a little bit of feeling in my fingers.

You've represented Australia in the Claxton Shield competition, the 2008 Olympics qualifier, and the 2009 World Baseball Classic. Is it important to you to continue representing your country even while you're pursuing baseball as a career over here?

I mean, obviously I love to represent my country, and it's one of the greatest honors you can do as an Australian, playing baseball in America, stuff like that. But the thing is, though, sometimes the tournaments run into the season, and it's tough to be able to get teams to let you get time off, and I know that the Twins are pretty good with that. But hopefully with the new Classic coming up, I think it's next year, hopefully I'll be able to go to that. We'll just see, it'll just depend on if I get invited to big league Spring Training camp and how everything like that goes.

123

I figured a lot of people who read our site might not be familiar with the Claxton Shield, so I was wondering if you could just explain what that is?

The Claxton Shield is like MLB over here, for Australia. It's like the top of the top in Australia playing over there. This year it changed into the Australian Baseball League and is now funded by Major League Baseball. So they're getting a lot of prospects sent out there last year, like one of our teammates, Brett Jacobson, was sent out to play with the Perth Heat as well as a couple of the Orioles guys as well. Each team has a couple of different guys from different organizations, and it was a really good competition this year. It was good to see it get up and started and the crowds that we had were really good.

Last year you had an excellent season between Beloit and Fort Myers. What was working for you last year?

I was just pounding the zone, like I was just throwing strikes, I was feeling strong and feeling good and I had all my pitches working for a lot of the year. And I was being able to throw all my offspeed for strikes and making hitters feel uncomfortable, which is a big part of the game. So I just was able to use that all at the same time and it just worked for me.

And you throw five pitches?

I throw a fastball, two-seam fastball, changeup, curveball, slider.

I think I'd read that you were messing around with a cutter a little bit.

Messing around, but it's not anything to write home about yet.

You haven't been in the Eastern League very long, you've only pitched a few times. What are your thoughts so far on the step up, as far as the competition goes, the quality of hitters?

Well, the weather's not my biggest friend at the moment, had a couple rainouts, but the competition of hitters is a lot harder. I've noticed that. You don't get away with as much. Like I've missed a couple spots and I've left a couple pitches over the middle and I've paid for it both times. So I mean, you've just got to go out there and keep the ball low and keep the hitters off your fastball and mix in the offspeed and stuff like that, just keep pounding the zone and staying ahead.

It seems like now, there's a lot more guys from Australia than ever before in the minor leagues and the major leagues. Do you guys kind of know each other, do you communicate while you're here?

A lot of the Australians know each other just from the Australian academy, like I said, that two month thing before, so a lot of people know each other from there, and if you're in the same organization you tend to stick together a little bit as well. But there's a couple of the older guys that you know of and they might know of you but you don't really talk to that often. But a lot of the guys do know each other and they keep talking to each other throughout the season.

Hendriks was 8-2 with a 2.70 ERA and 81 strikeouts for New Britain in the first half, earning a promotion to Rochester in mid-July. After 4-4 record in nine starts with the Red Wings, he was called up to Minnesota and made his Major League debut against Jake Peavy and the Chicago White Sox on September 6, allowing three runs on four hits in seven innings.

--Originally posted May 4, 2011 by Brian Moynahan

Chad Jenkins
New Hampshire Fisher Cats (Toronto Blue Jays)

Chad Jenkins was Toronto's first round pick (20th overall) out of Kennesaw State in the 2009 draft. He began the 2011 season, his second as a professional, at High-A Dunedin before earning a promotion to New Hampshire in June.

Jenkins sat down with me before this afternoon's game against the Portland Sea Dogs. We talked about his experience on draft day, how he spent the time in between the draft and when he actually signed, and how he develops his pitches.

First thing I wanted to ask about, I was reading in Baseball America just now, the Prospect Handbook, that when you were in college, the scouts that were onto you were onto one of your teammates first, and then from that you got a lot of attention. When did you start noticing that you were getting that attention?

Honestly, I got a little bit coming into my junior year, that summer ball, I started to get some scouts and stuff, but I didn't really think much of it. But I was throwing the ball really well, so I was hoping I could just take it into the fall at school and throw really well. Once we got to school, the other guy, [Kyle] Heckathorn, we went to fall practice and scouts started showing up and I guess I got my chance, and I took advantage of it.

Can you tell me a little about the whole experience of draft day?

It was really weird. Leading up to the draft, we were out of school, we had finished up school ball, and I didn't really do too much, just kind of hung out, not a whole lot going on. I went to a couple pre-draft workouts, so that was kind of fun. But about three or four days up to the draft, I didn't have anything to do. I just kind of hung out with friends and stuff, took it easy. And I remember on draft day, I actually went back to school, got a little workout in, hung out with some friends at school, and then went home. That night, my best friend came over, just me and my parents and my two best friends, and we just sat there and watched the draft.

And then obviously, first round. Were you expecting to go that high, or was that a little bit of a surprise?

It was a tossup where I was going to go. I wasn't really sure, cause I had talked to some people higher than that, and my agent kept texting me, "Just wait for so-and-so." Cause I was almost positive some after Toronto, but he was always like, "I'd watch out for Toronto at pick 20, I think they're going to take you." And sure enough, he was right.

And how long did it take you to sign after the draft?

About two months. It was kind of weird – didn't really get any extra money, anything like that. [*Ed. Note: According to the Baseball America Prospect Handbook, Jenkins signed for the recommended slot of $1.359 million.*] I got a couple of incentives that were nice, but that whole summer was fun. It was my first summer without baseball, and I took full advantage of it.

So you were like a typical kid coming out of college, before you had to go into the real world you got to kick back a little bit.

Yeah, I did. It was nice. I tried to work out every day, and that kept me in shape, cause I knew once I signed I'd have to go straight into it. But other than that, I just enjoyed being 21 [years-old]. It was nice. I didn't do anything crazy. I should fix that, when I said I enjoyed being 21. I didn't do anything crazy, I didn't go out and get drunk every night. I just enjoyed being a college kid and doing the summer. Played some golf here and there, hung out with friends a lot, just took life easy.

Now some of the stories I was reading just now, they mentioned your weight coming out of college, how you were working to control it, eat better. You looked like you were just busting your butt out there [we talked as he was coming off the field after a workout], but is that something you're still working on? Is that a constant part of your development as a player?

Right now, no it's not. Right now I'm happy. Coming out of college I was a little heavier, probably about 255, and then my first year of pro ball I came in at 220. And I didn't feel good playing at that weight. I wasn't happy with it, I felt sluggish some. So this offseason, I tried to put some of my weight back on and I got to a weight that I'm happy with. I'm about 240 right now and I'm really happy with that weight. It's lighter than I was in college, but heavier than my first full year in pro ball, so I feel like I've found a happy medium.

I want to talk a little bit about the pitches you're throwing. What I read was sinker, fastball, slider, changeup. From what I was reading, the sinker sounds like it's kind of unfair.

Yeah, it's been a good pitch for me. I learned it at a young age. I came from a small town – well, I came from a small baseball high school, and I played East Cobb in Georgia, which most people know. But I never really called it a sinker, I just called it my two-seam. I never thought anything of it. And then once I got to pro ball, everybody's like, "Yeah, it's a sinker, it's a sinker." And I got that just pounded into me.

It's been awesome. It's got me out of a lot of jams and it's helped me get deep into games.

How often do you throw that pitch in any given game?

A lot. That's my go-to. If I feel like I'm in trouble, I always go straight to it. Especially if it's on – if it's working, it's unbelievable. Now sometimes, you can't get it flat. That's when you start asking the umpire for a new ball [laughs].

How do you throw it? Is it just that the grip is different?

My grip's unique. I don't know too many people in pro ball that have it. I'm sure there are some, but for me, I put my two fingers directly in between the two seams. I don't touch any seams. Just in between the two and throw it like a fastball.

So I'm assuming that one was the first thing you threw when you were younger. So when did the other pitches enter the mix? The slider, the change?

The slider came around a lot in college. We worked on that a lot my sophomore and junior year and it really started to turn around for me. Changeups always been there, I grew up throwing a changeup, but I recently just changed the grip on the changeup, which has been HUGE for me. It actually got me out of a lot of jams the other night, cause I didn't really have a feel for my fastball so I had to find something else. Fortunately for me the changeup was there and it was unbelievable.

It's always hard for me to phrase this question, but how does the development of a pitch go? Like your slider – like, the way I look at it: Professional Pitcher, you pick up the ball and boom, you grip it and rip it and you got it. But how does it develop?

For me, it's the feel of my body. Like I'll know what my body feels like when it feels good, and as soon as I let one go I can tell you if it's going to be good or bad. So for me it's feel. And for me to learn a new pitch or fine tune one of my pitches, I have to know what it feels like to throw a good one, and to do it every time you just got to keep repeating. It's always, repeat your delivery, repeat your arm slot. For me, if I can repeat that every time, then it becomes ingrained, and you know what a good one feels like. That way you know how to get there and all that.

So are you making adjustments out there on the mound, saying, "Okay, that one didn't feel right, but I know what I have to do." Are you kind of tinkering with it on the mound or are you trying to just go on your muscle memory on the mound?

When you get on the mound, a lot of things go through your head, obviously. But for me, it's like if I feel something a little off, I'll tell myself, "Hey, slow down, stay behind the rubber. You're getting ahead of yourself, you're missing arm side, so you're getting quick." Just small things like that to help me stay focused on my path to the dish.

We hear now about the cutter being the new sort of "it" pitch. You know, everybody who's anybody is throwing a cutter. Is that something that you've thought about messing around with at all?

We kind of messed with it a little at the beginning of the year, and then I don't know what happened, it didn't bother me, but we decided to scrap it. But for me, my slider's hard, and so a lot of people call my slider a cutter. Cause I'll throw the slider hard. But no, the cutter's not for me.

So in a way you throw one, it's just a difference of the name?

It's harder with a little more depth. To be honest, when I think of a cutter, all I see in my head is Mo's cutter, [Mariano] Rivera's cutter, and all you see is 94 and straight across. So that's the only cutter I ever see. I've tried to throw that, but I just can't. My cutters are down and across. I call it my slider, some people call it a cutter. I just know I throw it hard.

Jenkins was 4-5 with a 3.07 ERA in 11 starts for Dunedin. Following his promotion to New Hampshire, he posted a 5-7 record and 4.13 ERA.

--Originally posted June 26, 2011 by Brian Moynahan

Mike McDade

New Hampshire Fisher Cats (Toronto Blue Jays)

Selected by the Toronto Blue Jays in the sixth round of the 2007 draft, 22-year-old Mike McDade has made a steady climb through the minor leagues, stopping at Low-A Lansing in 2009, High-A Dunedin in 2010, and Double-A New Hampshire this season. The big, switch-hitting first baseman has cooled off a bit after a hot start, but is still showing off some of the power that resulted in 37 homeruns combined over the past two seasons.

McDade sat down with me following a weekend in which the Fisher Cats played three games in two days totaling 23 innings, nearly eight hours of game time, and nearly four hours of rain delays. We talked about the worst weather to play in, the one time he played third base in the pros, and whether or not he's ever had to run over a catcher.

The first thing I wanted to say was that when I was looking up stuff, I noticed yesterday [May 8] was your birthday. So I felt like I had to wish you a happy belated birthday.

Appreciate it, thank you, thank you very much.

So you had the doubleheader yesterday. Did you do anything afterwards to get out and celebrate a little bit?

Nah. I mean, the day before we had a long day too, rain delay, but I just went back home to hang out with my other teammates and we just watched TV. Not too much. Just try to rest up and get ready for today.

It's a couple long days of baseball, huh?

Yeah…you got to do it, you got to love it. It's baseball. Rain? That happens during the season, you just got to adapt to it.

In listening to a couple interviews that you'd done before, I know you mentioned the rain and the weather a few times.

We've had a pretty crappy spring, as far as weather goes. Do you kind of view that as part of your development as a player, learning to handle whatever Mother Nature throws at you?

Oh yeah. You just got to figure out what works for you during rain delays, if it's playing cards, or listening to music, something, anything. Maybe getting a little workout in or something. You just got to find what's best for you. After coming from the Florida State League I've got a pretty good idea what to do during rain delays to stay ready for the game, stay focused for it.

What's the worst kind of weather to play in?

Worst weather? [long pause] I'm not a fan of playing in the freezing rain. I mean, it's already cold, then you've got rain hitting you sideways. It's just not too fun. I mean, I'm not much of a complainer. I'll go out there and play in anything. It's hard when it's cold and you've got rain just slapping you in the face, trying to catch the ball, trying to hit the ball. It's tough, but you got to do it.

You're off to a great offensive start, but what I wanted to ask you about first was your defense. It seems like every season so far in the pros you've improved. You went from 17 errors to 14 to 8, and this year, I don't think you've made an error yet. How much practice time are you putting in on defense?

Tremendous. Especially during BP, I try to get my work in every day, just to focus, just to catch the ball. That's the big thing for me over there, just catch the ball. I know I've got time. A little closer to first, I've got time to catch the ball, knock it down somehow, get rid of it and get the out. I focus on that. I used to be a catcher in high school. That kind of helped me be a first baseman, knowing that defense is a big part of it. I'm always defense first, you know, I'm always worried about my defense. I've got the confidence that my swing will be there, it's just defense I worry about, just trying to get better every day.

I used to play first base a LONG time ago – you were a baby when I was playing first base – and I think a lot of times it's kind of viewed as one of those positions that's kind of easy, just throw the big slow guy out there and he doesn't have to move around a lot. But obviously, there's technique to it, there's something to it. What is it, when you're out there in the field, what is it that you're looking at and thinking about, trying to get ready and position yourself?

That's the thing, when I first got drafted – I used to be a catcher, they drafted me as a first baseman – that's the same kind of mindset I had: it should be pretty easy over there, just go out there and swing it, but more and more every year I've learned that it's just as important a spot on the field as center, short, anywhere on the field. Just over there, just read the hops, just be alert, just know what you're going to do with the ball before you get it. Just be always a couple plays ahead. Just being alert over there.

Where do the errors come from when they happen?

Sometimes maybe just a lack of focus, not getting really down on the ball, keeping my eye there, just coming up. Errors happen. Sometimes throwing to second or sometimes throwing to first, just rushing it – it's that close – just rushing it. Knowing that I have time, relax, take your time, try to get the out. That's the biggest thing: I just start to rush, sometimes kind of panic. You make that first bobble, you still got time to pick it up. That's what happens.

So a variety of things that kind of get ironed out over time.

Yeah, like I said, work during BP, maybe some days early work, get out there and just fine-tune on some things, just keep a sharp grasp of everything.

133

When I was looking up your stats, correct me if I'm wrong, but it looked like every game you've played as a professional has been either at first base or at DH, except there was one game that I saw last year at Dunedin where you were listed at third base. How did that happen?

That was a weird day, just a lot of things happened. We were kind of short on players, couple guys hurt, and just happened I had to go play third for two innings, at least. I played third in high school so it wasn't something I wasn't used to, but I wish I would've got a ball. Of course, both innings the pitcher struck out the side. Of course, both innings. The only innings they strike out the side, when I'm at third. I remember, Anthony Gose, he was on the Phillies, and he tried to bunt on me. But he bunted foul. I keep on teasing him about that, like, "If you had got that down I would've thrown you out."

You were ready to make that play.

Yeah, yeah, I was ready. He tried to bunt on me, but no. I wish he would've got it fair, cause I would've thrown him out and embarrassed him. And I would've had that on him right now.

It was fun being on that side of the diamond. It's just a different world. You're playing always on first, you go over there on that side, it's just shook. It just shakes you up. It's like, "Wow, it's different over here." It was fun, it was fun, the two innings I played over there.

Don't want to do it all the time though?

I don't know, I always like to try different positions. Third base is somewhat similar to first, you know, it's the corners, you get hot shots, you got to be ready for anything, you got to be alert. But it'd be fun one day to venture out over there, one day, one game. Have a little fun.

Like I said, offensively you're off to a really great start this year. Your power numbers are down a little bit, it seems like, but it also seems like your strikeouts are down a little bit too so far. Was there any sort of conscious effort to cut down your strikeouts, coming into the year?

No, not really. It's just really more maturity, just getting a game plan going up to the plate. Sometimes, especially last year, I'd just go up there and try to swing, swing hard. Now I'm trying to focus, get my pitch, and do some damage on it. That's just the biggest thing, get a pitch that I can swing at and put a good swing on it, that's all I can ask for, barrel it up. So after that it's just wherever it goes.

Now, do you look at what your numbers are? Because I know when I talked to Anthony last week or the week before, his numbers showed that he was struggling, but he said he felt the best he had ever felt. Are you looking at your numbers or is it more concentrated on feel?

No, it's mostly on feel. You know, it's just all about development. Right now, I feel the best at the plate, because I'm swinging at strikes, not swinging at the balls in the dirt, not swinging out of my zone, not swinging at THEIR pitches, waiting to get MY pitch and put a good swing on it. So that's what I feel like is good for me, that I'm developing as a player. The numbers show up at the end of the year. If I can develop keep that during the whole year, consistency, is the big thing.

Now, you're not a guy who's known for your speed. And a couple weeks ago, you scored, you were on first, there was a double – I wasn't actually here, I didn't see it – you came around all the way from first. On a play like that – and I can sympathize, I'm a big dude myself, I get tired quick – you're coming into third, Sal's waving you in…is there anything in the world that's going to stop you from scoring at that point?

No. I mean, it's pretty hard to stop this, it's hard to shut it down. Once I'm going, I'm pretty much gone. It's a far way from first to home, but it's nice sometimes to get all the way around because most of the time you're really not scoring from that far. You feel fast, running from first to home. You feel like, "Yeah, I did something." But it's all good. I like doing the bases, I love running the bases. It's a good feeling, just trying to help the team win any possible way.

Have you ever been coming in and had to run over a catcher?

No, I haven't had that chance to. It'll probably come sooner or later. It's going to be where I just can't stop. It's not really I'm going to try to blow him up, it's going to be bang bang boom. It's going to happen, hopefully the guy don't get hurt too bad. Or me, myself. So I haven't had a chance to do that yet, but we'll see.

From what I've heard you're pretty relaxed and easygoing – I can kind of tell from talking to you, you're a pretty relaxed, easygoing guy – in the clubhouse. How much of that do you take to the field with you? Cause you hear a lot about guys sometimes who are loose in the clubhouse and they get out on the field and they're a monster. You know, you don't talk to them. But then they get back off the field and they're the nicest guy in the world. How much does that relaxed mindset help?

It's huge. To play this game, you got to be relaxed. You can't be tense all the time. It might work for a few people, but it just doesn't work for me. During the game I'm pretty serious, but you can always come up and talk to me, I won't just not talk to you if I'm having a bad day or something like that. You can always ask me anything. I'm just relaxed. Just play this game, have fun with it. Something we'll be doing for six months, might as well have fun doing it.

McDade hit .281 with 16 homeruns and 74 RBI in 125 games for New Hampshire and won the Homerun Derby at the Eastern League All-Star Game in July. Defensively, he made seven errors in 973 chances for a .993 fielding percentage. He did not have a chance to play a position other than first base.

--Originally posted May 17, 2011 by Brian Moynahan

Mike Minor
Gwinnett Braves (Atlanta Braves)

Selected by the Atlanta Braves with the 7th overall pick in the 2009 Draft, 23-year-old Mike Minor has been blazing a trail directly to the majors. After a rocky start in Rome and Mississippi, Minor made a name for himself last season when he was called up to Triple-A Gwinnett. The 6-foot-3, 210-pound lefty took some time after a recent start to talk about his pitching, being a highly touted prospect, and how he has been able to keep his focus along the way.

Looked like you had some control problems tonight with the four walks, what went wrong?

Lack of concentration I guess, Just didn't really feel it tonight, the cold weather was giving my hands a little bit of a dry feeling, that's not an excuse at all. Just had lack of control pretty much the whole game until the very end, then I settled down a little bit.

During the game the manager decided to change catchers, did that throw you off at all?

No, not at all because I've thrown to both of them. Both of them you can talk to, work with you, they both have a good game plan.

Is there a lot of pressure on you each start being such a highly regarded prospect?

No, because the coaches don't put it on me, the players don't put it on me, the organization doesn't put it on me, and I don't put it on myself. I don't say "Hey if I don't do good this start than they aren't going to call me up." I mean I don't even put that in my head. I put it more "Do I feel good?" or "Are we going to win tonight for the team", as long as they have my back I have theirs.

Going forward this season, what do you feel you need to improve on?

138

Just the walks, control has been a little bit of an issue. Other than that my four pitches have been coming along nicely. The curve ball I used to struggle with a little bit here and there, now it's pretty much there every game, the last three starts have been a lot of swing and misses on it, first pitch strikes with it. The slider is just an okay pitch right now that I picked up about two weeks ago. I'm still getting misses off of it, first inning I struck out the three hole guy, so both of them are coming along. The changeup for the most part has been there the whole time.

Are there any goals that you are setting for the season? Obviously at some point I'm sure you are hoping to get called up, but while you are here what are your goals - help the team win an International League championship?

Yeah I mean, that's one of the goals...I'm not really a stat guy, so I don't really do the ERA, the strikeouts, the WHIP, all that stuff, I don't even look at that. Mostly just do it off how I feel, and how I can help out the team, whatever team I'm on. If I do get called up, I get called up, but right now it's this team. The Gwinnett Braves are who I am trying to pitch for.

Is it tough not to listen to people talk about you? Your name has been floating around early on this season... how do you ignore it?

I tell my parents not to say anything, I tell my friends not to say anything, so I really don't hear it. I really don't hear what they say as long as no one else in the clubhouse comes up to me, I really don't tell people in the clubhouse, "Hey don't come up to me." The guys in the clubhouse know better, they won't say anything to me. My teammates really know the game, they've been around for a little bit. This isn't Low-A ball, these guys aren't just getting drafted, they've been around...they know the game and they know what to say. I just shut that out, all the other personal stuff I just shut it out.

Obviously there are guys who you've come up through the Braves system with, is there a certain connection that you keep with them to keep you level headed?

Yeah for the most part I've been level headed, since I was drafted. People may say things, "He did this" or "He showed him up", but if I did or I was doing that I don't mean to come off that way...sometimes people say "Oh he's quiet" or "He's cocky" but I'm just a quiet guy. I really try not to say much, I try to be low key, and sometimes guys take that the wrong way. All the guys that I've met throughout the organization have been real nice to me, and have accepted me since the first day.

Minor was 4-5 with a 3.13 ERA in 16 starts for Gwinnett. He struck out 99 batters and walked 27 in 100.2 innings. He returned to the Major Leagues after making his debut last August, starting 15 games and compiling a 5-3 record, 4.14 ERA, and 77/30 K/BB ratio in 82.2 innings.

--Originally posted May 17, 2011 by Chris Fee

Stolmy Pimentel
Portland Sea Dogs (Boston Red Sox)

Stolmy Pimentel is the sixth-ranked prospect in the Boston Red Sox system according to the Baseball America Prospect Handbook. The 21-year-old right-hander has progressed steadily through the minors, spending full seasons at every level from Rookie to High-A. He is off to a rough start with Double-A Portland this season, with an 0-4 record and 7.06 ERA entering last night's game against New Hampshire, but has shown flashes of brilliance, such as the five innings of two-hit ball against New Britain on April 15 or his performance against the Fisher Cats.

Pimentel took a few minutes to speak with me after the game (which his Sea Dogs lost, 1-0, on a walk-off single by Moises Sierra in the bottom of the ninth) about the origins of his outstanding changeup, what goes through his mind when he gets in a jam, and the benefit of playing in a small league.

First of all, you had a great outing tonight – six innings, three hits, one walk, seven strikeouts. You've struggled a little bit, so how did tonight feel different from some of your other outings so far?

Tonight I was just thinking about trying to compete, trying to do my best. I know my last start wasn't too good, but I wasn't thinking about that. I was thinking about, let's go to work, let's go to compete, try to do my best, and I felt very good today. I felt aggressive and confident with all my pitches, so I feel like that's what I have to try to keep doing.

I read that you're working on consistency with your curve and command of your fastball. Did you feel like those were really working for you tonight?

Yeah, yeah, my fastball was really good today. I had very good command today with my fastball and my changeup and my curveball too, I threw a couple very good curveballs. And that's

141

about it, to keep working and keep developing my fastball and my other pitches.

What was your pitch selection like tonight? What did you throw, the most to least?

I threw a lot of fastballs and a lot of changeups today. I have a really good feeling about my pitches, what I was trying to do was to make nice pitches, to just throw strikes and try to make outs.

It seemed like there were a couple innings where you kind of went away from your fastball a little bit and were trying to throw more of the offspeed stuff.

Yeah [smiles]. Those times, that happens when you have a very good feeling with your second pitch, you know? But I don't like to forget about my fastball, I like to use my fastball, but sometimes the game's telling you, the situation is like you have to do this or you have to throw that, you know, and that was what I was trying to do. Try to make outs no matter what pitch. I felt very good today with all my pitches, so…

Baseball America says you actually have the best changeup in the whole Red Sox system. Where did you learn that, where does that come from?

[smiles] I think I just had a feeling for it. Because before I signed I was a shortstop, so I started pitching when I was 16-years-old. So I signed when I was 16-years-old and a couple months, so I guess I had a feeling for my changeup. Nobody told me, "You have to do this, you have to do this." No, I just threw it.

In the sixth inning tonight, you got into a little bit of a jam. You had guys on first and third, I think, two outs. What are you thinking about out there? Are you just thinking about getting that last out, just what you can do to get the guy at the plate?

Yeah, I was trying to get the out. I was thinking about nobody can beat me, I'm better than the hitter, so I'm going to try to do my best right here, and that was whatever happened. I tried to focus on that hitter and I said, "Okay, let's go. Let's get him." And I was very positive, and I was thinking, "I'm better than the hitter. Let's go, let's get this guy out, nobody's going to score on me tonight." Tonight I feel like it's my day, so let's go, let's do it.

This is your fifth professional season, and every year you've gone up exactly one level. How does the level you were at last year, High-A, compare to Double-A so far? Or even to some of the other steps you've taken?

The difference is every time you go up to another level, you see better hitters. You see better stuff, better pitchers, better hitters, and I think that's the difference. Because it's the same baseball, but you see a lot of better hitters. They don't swing far away. They like to hit a good pitch, you know? I think that's the difference.

And part of the challenge last year was the size of the league, is one thing I've seen. It was such a small league that you were in, you may say the same team two or three or four times. And you've run into that a couple times already this season. How does that experience, facing the same team two or three times, how does that help you become a better pitcher?

I think that helps because if you see a team a couple times, you can have the idea how those hitters are, if they have a long swing, or they have a short swing, or if they like to take pitches. Things like that help a lot because you can have better [unintelligible] with a hitter. So I think that helps you.

And the last thing: you played in the Futures Game last year, represented the Red Sox, what was the best part of that experience for you?

That was amazing [smiles]. That was like if you were in the big leagues, you know? Because everything was so, so, so good, everything was like real big league, the big show. I enjoyed it, to be over there, and be with other players from other teams. That was very good to be over there.

Were there guys that you talked to about where they're at and what they're learning? Did you compare notes with some of the other players?

Not really, because when I was over there I was just trying to enjoy the moment, waiting for my chance to have the ball and show what I got. So I wasn't thinking about, "Oh, what did the guy do?" or what this guy has. I was thinking about enjoying myself, to have the ball and do my job.

After beginning the season 0-9 with a 9.12 ERA for Portland, Pimentel was sent back to the Red Sox High-A affiliate in Salem, where he finished 6-4 with a 4.53 ERA, struck out more hitters, and walked fewer.

--Originally posted May 10, 2011 by Brian Moynahan

D'Vontrey Richardson

Brevard County Manatees (Milwaukee Brewers)

Brewers farmhand and current Brevard County Manatee D'Vontrey Richardson is not only the Brewers 24th-ranked prospect according to Baseball America, but also a former Florida State University two-sport athlete. During his time at FSU (2007-2009), he played centerfield for the baseball team and was a backup quarterback on the Seminole football team.

During a recent visit to Tampa to play the Tampa Yankees, I caught up with D'Vontrey and we talked baseball, the transition from FSU to the minors, and whether or not he sees alumni pulling for him throughout the state of Florida.

Let's start with some "getting to know you"-type questions. What is your favorite sports movie?

Favorite sports movie ... hmm. Probably "The Longest Yard."

The first one or the second one?

The second one.

Who are your favorite all-time athletes?

I don't have many, but probably Vick football-wise. In baseball, probably Gary Sheffield. Whenever I was growing up, I would see him play. In basketball, probably (Derrick) Rose now, with how explosive he is.

Now, wait, The Longest Yard, that's the movie with Burt Reynolds in the original, right? How can you like the second one more? You stayed in Burt Reynolds Hall, right? Burt might not be too happy.

[Laughs] Right. Well, I ain't seen the first one. I've only seen the second one.

145

You were injured earlier this season. How is the hip?

It's better. It comes with the game. Just trying to play. I have to get stronger and try to stay in the lineup. It was a struggle initially as it was my first real injury. So I am trying to get out there and do something.

You are warming up at the plate after a slow start. What's going right?

Just bunting, actually. I'm still not seeing the ball the way I want to, but that's baseball. You have a lot of ups and downs. I'm just trying to battle through the struggle. I feel like I am still not seeing the ball like I should, so it's just relaxing and bunting and trying to get myself some confidence.

You say you are not seeing the ball the way you should. What are you doing to try to help that out?

Just taking it day by day. Because all it takes is one swing. Just seeing the ball more, I guess. You're going to be cold, you're going to be hot, and more times cold, so I got to learn how to battle through that cold streak.

I'd like to talk to you about your 6-for-6 day a couple of months ago.

That was a little bit of luck. The night before that, I went 1-for-4 and hit every ball on the barrel. The day after that, I hit one ball on the barrel and that was a double, and then everything else I hit on the end of the bat, I got jammed and all, and the hits just came. That's the game. It was a little bit of luck but I took it.

Did it help the confidence out a little?

It helped me out. Especially with the series after that, I was starting to feel good.

146

So what adjustments did you make this year over your first year last season?

Just mentally. Last year was my first full season of just baseball. I couldn't deal with the struggles, but this year I've adjusted to it, understanding that it is just part of the game.

What are your goals for this year?

My goals for this year are to finish strong, start fresh, and get stronger in the offseason. To try to stay healthy through to the offseason so I can get stronger.

So I have a few background questions for you. Why did you choose baseball over football?

Well, it was an opportunity that opened. I was playing both football and baseball there and my whole life people were telling me that I was going to have to choose, so it just came and I felt like I had to take it.

Did you see (fellow former FSU two-sport athlete) Taiwan Easterling signed with Chicago?

Oh, he did? Which Chicago team?

The Cubs. Have you talked to him? Did you have any advice for him?

No, I haven't talked to him at all. But he got drafted fifth round out of high school before so he could be good. I mean, he is a great competitor. He is going to compete. He is going to continue to get better every day. But I haven't talked to him. The last time I talked to him was in February before Spring Training and he said he was going to leave. So congrats to him and I wish the best for him.

Did you talk to anyone in regards to your own decision to play baseball over football? Did you talk with Coach Bowden or Coach Martin?

Not particularly. They kind of thought I was going to take it anyway.

How is life in the minors versus life at Florida State?

It's different. I mean, it's more laid back. All the road trips. Not really at a custom place to stay. It's different, but I guess that's why they say the minor leagues is more mental. It's a grind. But at Florida State, you know, everything was basically taken care of. It was a D1 college, and they had good locker rooms and everything was nice there. It wasn't bad at all.

You hear a lot that Coach Bowden is very influential in people's lives. What have you brought with you from your time playing for him?

The years I was there he always preached God to us. To put God first and make sure you always have God in your life. That's one of the main things that I have with me now. To have that in mind, because he was always preaching that.

Ok, what about Coach Martin?

Same really. When he coached, he had a drive to him. He always wanted us to get better. So it's just something I learned there was to keep trying to get better.

Did you watch the baseball team or the football team this season?

No, no I didn't.

Ok, you mentioned you stayed in touch a bit with Taiwan. Is there anyone you still stay in touch with regularly?

On the football team, no one anymore. But baseball, yeah. I still know Sherman (Johnson, FSU third baseman), Hunter (Scantling, pitcher), (pitcher Brian) Busch, Tyler Everett (pitcher), Devon Travis (infielder). I talk to a couple of people. That's all I usually talk to when I go back, not many people.

Now that you are in the Florida State League, do you get many alumni who recognize you and pull for you?

I haven't really talked to too many, no.

I find that interesting, because when I looked at the Manatees roster, your name jumped out and I said to myself, "I should talk to him".

So is it a struggle in any way to put your Florida State background behind you? Do you want to be known as just a Brewers outfielder?

Yeah, I just want to be known as a Brewers outfielder and a baseball player. I mean, I didn't really do too much at Florida State. It's a great school and great coaches, but I had to take an opportunity here.

I totally understand that. Were you surprised when you were drafted?

Yeah, because I didn't get a chance to really prove myself. But obviously they saw something in me and they took me. And I am grateful for that.

In his second professional season in 2011, Richardson hit .284 with three homeruns and 41 RBI in 97 games. Defensively, he recorded 11 assists in centerfield.

--Originally posted July 13, 2011 by Mike Lortz

Moises Sierra
New Hampshire Fisher Cats (Toronto Blue Jays)

One of the players I've looked forward to speaking with all season is New Hampshire Fisher Cats outfielder Moises Sierra. Possibly the strongest player on the team, this season Sierra has hit a ball off the Hilton Garden Inn in left-center field and delivered three walk-off base hits.

This was the third interview I've done with a player who did not speak English as his first language and the second in which we did not use a translator. It was interesting to note that on at least one question, Sierra wanted to explain himself in greater detail but could not find the words in English to say what he was thinking. That's not to take anything away from him — he was excellent, and the time and effort he put into our conversation was much appreciated. Like most (if not all) of the players I've dealt with this season, he seems like a genuinely nice young man.

Also worth noting about Sierra: I originally attempted to set up this interview last week, before the team left on a road trip, but he was unavailable before the game because he was doing extra work in the batting cage. After we spoke in the clubhouse on Wednesday, I went across the field to do another interview. As I headed back to the press box afterward, less than an hour before game time, I passed Sierra underneath the stands as he walked into the batting cage. He certainly puts in some work.

Can you tell me a little about when you started playing baseball?

When I was younger, I played baseball in Little League. I started playing baseball when I was eight years old.

Two things you're known for are your power and your throwing arm. When did you realize that those were special?

When I was 14-years-old, I had a good arm. I threw a lot, long toss. And my power hitting is natural, you know, from my father. My father is strong too.

Did your dad play baseball also?

Not really, no. As a little kid, just a little.

Did he teach you about the game?

No, I had coaches. The coaches taught me about baseball, about everything.

Earlier this season, I didn't see it, but I heard you hit a ball that hit the hotel.

Yeah [laughs].

When you hit a ball like that, how does it feel, physically?

When I hit the ball, I don't feel nothing. I don't feel the contact, you know? That's good contact. And I feel very excited, happy.

You have three walkoff hits this year, to end games. Is there something about that situation where it's a close game, it's late – do you focus more, or is every at-bat the same?

Yeah, yeah. In that situation, I'm more focused, more concentration, and I go up to the plate looking to make good contact. And that's it. Concentration.

Just going up there and getting a pitch to hit.

Exactly. I'm looking for a good pitch and trying to hit a line drive.

Last year you were hurt a lot of the year. How did you handle the frustration of not being able to play? Was it hard to have to sit on the sidelines, sit on the bench, and just watch?

I got surgery on my hand, the hamate bone, and only played like eight games. It's hard because I want to play, you know? You want to play and that's difficult because you're hurt and you can't do nothing. You're watching the game and you think, "Wow, I want to play." And you can't play.

So it's just frustrating.

Exactly. I got two fractures – my hand and my leg. In Spring Training, my leg was broken. When I started hitting, my hand was sore and swollen.

So you thought you were finally ready to play, and then you get hurt again.

Exactly. That's a bad year.

In 2007, that was your first season in America. How difficult was it to adjust from playing and living in the Dominican Republic?

That's different. My first time was difficult because it's another country, you know, and the way they play in the Dominican is different from here. The baseball is harder.

Like the quality of players?

Quality of players. There are a lot of players here, too. Different country. The baseball here is harder.

Do you feel you've come a long way since then, four years ago? Do you feel like you've gotten used to it, to the culture and the baseball?

Now it feels normal. Like two years ago, I felt nervous. [long pause] It's difficult.

In 2009 you came here to Manchester for a few games. Were you excited to come back this season?

Oh yeah, very excited, because this league is Double-A. This league is hard, it's good baseball, and you're close to the big leagues [laughs]. I like it here.

What do you do to work on your English?

You know what, my first year, I spoke no English. I said no to English. And the next year I picked up a little bit, and this year is better. I speak it with my teammates, and I talk a lot with the American players. I practice my English. I talk about everything.

Sierra hit .277 with 18 homeruns and 67 RBI in 133 games for New Hampshire. He finished second to teammate Mike McDade in the Homerun Derby at the Eastern League All-Star Game and recorded 11 outfield assists. He nearly added another game-winning hit to his resume in the playoffs, homering to give New Hampshire a temporary lead in the eighth inning of Game 1 of the League Championship Series.

--Originally posted July 8, 2011 by Brian Moynahan

Michael Spidale
Reading Phillies (Philadelphia Phillies)

During the Eastern League All-Star Game, I had a seat next door to the radio booth. I could hear everything they were saying, and at one point, New Hampshire broadcaster Bob Lipman mentioned that Reading's Michael Spidale had played in Double-A for all or part of the last five seasons.

That piqued my interest, so when Reading came to town, I resolved to speak with Spidale. I was told that he doesn't do a lot of interviews and might be willing to give me a couple minutes after batting practice; after an initial attempt to flag him down failed, I caught his attention and he gave me 15 minutes. We spoke about staying motivated, how a good player stays consistent, and his role as a leader in the clubhouse.

Is it more frustrating, or more annoying, to be at one level for five years, or to have people constantly asking you if you're frustrated for being at one level for five years?

I'd say it's frustrating. I don't know about annoying, I don't think that would be the right word to use, but it can get frustrating at times. Especially when you're playing good ball, too, because when you're playing good ball you figure maybe you have a chance to move. But the game of baseball, when you've been playing for a while you see how it is, and it's a business like any other business.

Personally, I get asked that question a lot, like you said, "Is it frustrating? Is it annoying?" It is to a certain degree, but it's not, also, because you can't get overly frustrated. You can't get overly annoyed or think everyone's against you because that's not the way you should go about your game and about your business. Because when you do that, your play is going to suffer. You're going to be worried about how come I'm not here, how come I'm not there, how come I'm not getting a chance. And then you're going to be thinking about that rather than playing your game and playing hard and leaving it all on the field.

154

That's one thing that I can honestly say that I make a conscious effort to do, is not worry about stuff that's not in my control and worry about my game.

Where does the motivation to keep playing ball come from?

That's a good question. Sometimes it's tough, 'cause you got to be motivated, to play your best ball, to be at your tip-top game, you got to be motivated. I'm a huge believer in motivation. If you're not motivated you're not going to play to the best of your ability. And it is tough sometimes. I think my motivation is I like to play well. I'm not satisfied, it's not acceptable for me to go out there and half-ass it or have horse-shit numbers. I like to play well. If I said I was 0-for-4 and I came home and told you that I didn't care, I'd be lying to you. I like to play well, so I think that's my motivation, is I play my game and I want to succeed.

This is your 12th year. How many more years do you think you've got left?

I don't know, that's a good question. The last couple years I've thought about it, I've thought about, "This is it, this is it." That thought crosses your mind, and the last couple years it has. I don't know how many more years. I've never put a time limit on it.

It's never been like, "Oh, I want to play 15 years"?

No, no, no, I never did that. The last couple years I've just taken it year by year, see what happens, play the season out and see what happens at the end of the season. And I guess I'll do the same thing this year. I have decent numbers and I assume that some team will probably want to sign me. If I sign, I don't know, you know what I mean? I don't know. I'll take it day by day. I'll finish the year out, we've got a month and a half left. Play hard for that amount of time and see what the offseason brings. I'm not sure, but that's a good question, and it's something I've thought about.

What's the plan for when you are done?

I don't know yet. I don't have a specific plan, I've got a couple things in mind, but I don't have a specific thing to fall back on right now. I want to be around the game in some aspect, I don't know exactly what aspect. I don't know if I would want to be a professional coach, but baseball's in my blood so I know I'm going to have to be around the game in some respect, 'cause I'll probably go insane if I wasn't. Probably what I would say is I'm going to have my own something, my own business.

Like some batting cages or something?

Yeah, something like that. Maybe not even baseball. But whatever it's going to be, I'm going to have my own something.

You mentioned taking it year to year. If it came down to it, you finish up the year and you don't get any offers from affiliated teams – I saw you played independent ball a few years ago. Is that something you'd go back to, if you weren't ready to give it up?

No, I don't think so. I wouldn't play. I've been through that path already. I've done that. That would be it, that would be it. I don't think I would play indy ball. Indy ball, it's a lot of fun, but honestly the money's not there. The money's not there. I have a wife and a little baby now, so that would be something to think about, obviously.

Years ago when you went there, what was your mindset going in? You'd been with the White Sox for a few years. Where were you at mentally?

My mindset then, I was 24-years-old, was to get back into affiliated ball. That was my mindset. Went there, I was in Kansas

City, in the Northern League. That was my mindset: play well and try to get back with a team, see what happens. And it happened pretty quick. I was only there maybe a month and then the Phillies signed me.

Indy ball was a lot of fun, though. Indy ball was fun. If I didn't have a wife and kid, and nothing in affiliated ball, let's say next year in affiliated ball there was no opportunity or whatever, I would go play indy ball.

If you didn't have the financial responsibilities.

For sure, for sure, I would go play. It's fun, it's baseball. Good players, good players. It's equivalent to Double-A, Triple-A as far as talent. I would go do it. But sometimes, circumstances change.

I was originally going to ask you what's different this year, because I noticed you made the All-Star team for the first time. That was my question, then I went back and looked at your numbers and I realized that for the last few years you've been pretty consistent. And talking with some of the guys in short season leagues and some of the younger guys here, that's something that they're striving for, is consistency. So how do you get to that level and maintain that level?

That's probably the biggest thing, first of all, with being a good baseball player, is consistency, because everybody here can play. You know, you go down to short season, they all got talent. You can just close your eyes and pick a kid – if he's hot at that time, he's going to hit. He's going to go up there, he's going to get two hits, he's going to get three, or whatever. He's going to hit. But the question is, can he stay consistent? The question is, when he doesn't feel good at the plate, can he go 1-3 with a walk? And that's what it is about, because when you're playing every day, you don't feel the same at the plate every day. You don't feel great every day. Some days you do, some days you don't. The question is, what do you do on those days when you don't feel great? If your swing feels a little iffy, what do you do?

It's about adjustments, and I feel I'm really good at making adjustments pitch to pitch. If I feel something or if I see something then I'm able to nip it in the bud quick if it's something not good. Basically it's about adjustments. Adjustments and also mental attitude. The mental attitude is so important as a hitter because it's so hard. It's so hard to do and you fail so often that you need to be strong mentally to not get down on yourself, because if it gets up here [in your head], then it can screw you. And then your 0-for-4 game can turn into an 0-for-a series, rather than an 0-for-4 game and then boom, you bounce back with two the next day. See what I'm saying? And that's just mental, being strong mentally and being able to not let negatives affect you in the present. Always be in the present.

And the last thing I would say is experience. When I was younger, I went 1-for-69 one time, when I was 21-years-old. Now that's nothing physical, that's mental. I was screwed up in the head. And the more experience you get, the more at-bats you get, the better you are at that and the consistency will come out more. So those are the three things. I would say mental toughness, making adjustments, and experience.

As one of the older guys on the team, what is your role as a clubhouse leader?

I mean, it's pretty big. I think it's fair to say that I'm probably the leader on the team. And I'm happy about that. I like being a leader. I'm not a huge vocal leader. I will be if I have to. I'm a leader in leading by example. You know, if you go out there and bust your butt, play your game, play hard every day. And you got to play well, too, to earn some respect. You got to do that first, you got to take care of that first. Lead by example and then if you need to get vocal, you can get vocal, if you see something.

We got a great group of guys here. The young kids work hard, and we mesh well in the clubhouse, the clubhouse is nice. We have fun, which you need to do.

That's pretty much my role on the team. Like I said, I like leading by example. I've been playing for a number of years now, had no big league experience, and you get some 20-, 21-, 22-year-old kids here that are prospects, that are working their way up, first time through, and I would like to be a good influence on them. I'd like for them to look at me and say, "Look how he plays. That's how we should play." And I think they do, so I'm happy about that. If a kid's a hard worker – obviously they've got the talent – if he's a hard worker, I'll do anything I can to help him.

You guys had Shane Victorino and Brad Lidge with you last week. What does that do for you, how does that benefit you as a player, having guys around who have been up in the major leagues, who have that experience?

Nothing, really. It's cool to have them, but we can play down here too. We play good ball down here too. You put us up there, some guys will succeed. Some guys won't, some guys will. But it's nice having them. They're good guys, they're classy guys. They come down, and any rehab guy when I've been in Philly that's come down has been classy and carried themselves like a true major leaguer. So it is nice to see that. And they're hard workers as well. That's something that probably for the young guys is good to see, that those guys are in the big leagues making all that money and got the fame and stuff but they still get to work and work hard. That's important for them to see that that's how those guys go about their business, and Brad and Shane both did that, so that was nice to see. It was a nice few days in Trenton when they were there. You eat better too [laughs].

Spidale hit .326 for Reading this season, the second-best mark in his 12-year career. He stole more than 20 bases for the ninth time and in July was named to the Eastern League All-Star Game, his first such appearance.
--Originally posted July 22, 2011 by Brian Moynahan

Zach Stewart
New Hampshire Fisher Cats (Toronto Blue Jays)

Blue Jays right-hander Zach Stewart was the organization's number one prospect entering the 2010 season. He slipped to number six in 2011 (third among pitching prospects behind Kyle Drabek and Deck McGuire) and returned to Double-A New Hampshire for the second consecutive season.

Zach and I previously spoke last August, making this the first follow-up interview from The Bus Leagues Experience. We sat down last week prior to the Fisher Cats game against the Binghamton Mets and talked about the advantages of knowing your role on the pitching staff, the mental aspect of developing his changeup, and the importance of a good pitcher-catcher relationship.

You've started every game that you've appeared in since the start of last season, whereas before they were kind of moving you around, limiting your innings a little bit. Is it good for you to settle into that role, as opposed to moving back and forth between the bullpen and the rotation?

Yeah, I think it's good for anybody, in any situation, for them to get into a certain role and go with it. I think sometimes it gets to be hectic. And like in my case, I had success with both, but I think sometimes it can be mentally draining having to go back and forth, just with the different routines and things of that nature. It's still pitching, but there is a lot of difference in relief pitching and starting. So I think it does help because it lets you get into a rhythm, you get more used to it, so as far as that goes, anything when you get into it and you get going you get more of a rhythm, you get used to it, it helps more.

It's like you always hear about bullpen guys in the major leagues, they always say a guy likes to know if he's a sixth inning guy or an eighth inning guy.

Right, it kind of gives you a job description, almost, like, "This is what you got to do." It's not like, "Well, one day…" And I know that some guys have made careers out of it, and some guys you see back and forth and do well, but some guys, on the other hand, you can tell it takes a toll on them and they struggle with it. So yeah, I think with me it helps just getting settled in and having a clear-cut idea of what it is I'm supposed to be doing.

Now, two years in a row you've been a starter, but you've also gotten off to kind of a rough start in the league. Are some of the same factors you dealt with last season affecting you this season? The weather…?

No, I think the weather's affecting everybody right now. Seems like every couple days we're playing a doubleheader or something. I mean, it's not bad, it's just been really wet up here. But other than that nothing really stands out.

A lot of the hitters I've talked to, they say…like Anthony [Gose]. I talked to Anthony when his numbers showed that he wasn't really hitting well, and he was like, "Man, I feel great, it's just clicking for me. It's going to come." Do you feel kind of the same way, like your numbers may not reflect how you're feeling?

Yeah, I definitely feel that way. I feel like overall my arm feels good, all my stuff seems to be working the way it should. I just think it's one of those things. I had a start similar to this last year and then got into a rhythm, and then put together eight, ten good starts, and that pretty much made my season. So I'm thinking I feel good. I don't have any reason to worry. It's not like I'm looking at my numbers and sitting there thinking, "Oh man, this is a disaster." I feel good. I'm really not a big numbers guy anyway, so mostly I'm just going on how I feel. My last two starts *[Ed Note: five runs on 10 hits in five innings on May 7 and five runs on nine hits in six innings on May 12]* haven't been great, but they weren't terrible. I still felt like we were in the game when I got pulled and I ended up going, I think the last two games, if I remember, both of them were five or six innings apiece. So I'm getting my innings. Of course when you get out there every time you want to go out there and throw zeroes, but these guys we're playing against, it's tough to do that, day in and day out.

What pitches are you throwing now? What types of pitches?

I'm still a sinkerball guy. I throw my two-seamer a lot and try to get ground ball outs. I haven't really changed my approach as far as that goes, but I've always been a sinker-slider guy and that's pretty much what I'm still going with, and still working on the changeup. I think it's coming along a lot. I feel like it's a good pitch and I can use it. The more and more I throw it the more comfortable I get with it and the better it gets.

How does the development of a pitch like that – like, you picked up a change in the last few years?

Yeah.

How does the development of a pitch like that compare to the development of a pitch like your sinker, like your slider? Did those other two come naturally, did you have a feel for them?

Yeah, those were pitches I threw forever. A changeup, to me, has been a harder pitch to mentally grasp, because you're throwing a ball up there slow, and basically saying, "Here it is." You know, you're deceiving the hitter in a way, but in my mind, everything else I throw is hard or it breaks or it's moving down, and so it's like, "Okay, it has movement on it, this guy, if he puts the bat on it, he can get out." To me, the hardest part about getting used to throwing the changeup is, I'm basically throwing a cookie up there. Even though it is deceiving, if they do sit on it, it's an easy pitch to hit. That's how I looked at it. But from the hitter's point of view, it's actually probably the hardest pitch to adjust to in baseball. But as a pitcher, for me, it was hard to see it that way.

It kind of goes against your mentality.

Right. I'm throwing that ball up there to get crushed, is what I was thinking. But I've gotten used to it and thrown it in a lot of situations, and I've finally gotten to see that this isn't as easy for them to hit as it feels like. It's actually a tough pitch for them to get a grasp on and get a look at.

So when did you start working on the change as a third option?

I started working on it in college. It was just one of those things where, to me and my game plan, I never really had to use it as much because I had a good slider and I threw the ball pretty hard, and I could just blow the ball by people or get people swinging at a slider in the dirt, where in pro ball I kind of needed a third pitch, especially after I got out of the bullpen. In the bullpen it wasn't a big deal – fastball, slider, you're fine – but once I got out of the bullpen and realized, I got to start throwing five, six, seven, eight innings, you kind of need a third pitch, just something else for them to have to worry about.

What was it about the change? What was it that led you in that direction as opposed to a different third pitch?

I guess it's just that's the pitch. Pretty much if you talk to anyone, that's the starter pitch, that's the pitch that separates starters from relievers, or good starters from mediocre starters. That's just one more pitch for them to look at. It resembles a fastball so much that it IS hard for the hitter to have an idea of what's coming. They see fastball out of your hand 'cause it's hard for them to tell within that 60-feet-6-inches that it's going to be an offspeed pitch. It just looks like a fastball coming out of your hand, so it's tough for them to do anything with.

And you said as a starter versus a reliever, coming out of the bullpen you're going with just those two pitches.

Yeah, oh yeah, out of the bullpen I was just a slider-fastball guy. I throw a four-seam fastball as well, so I guess that's a different pitch in a way, but I was pretty much fastball-slider all the time. I didn't really mess with my changeup.

Is there a difference in the effort level between the two, where you're coming out to maybe throw an inning or two, how much you're putting into every pitch?

Oh yeah, yeah. To me, it's totally different. It's a totally different mindset. As a starter I'm trying to keep myself contained, keep myself within myself, just go out there, make my pitches, hit my spots. As a reliever, I would get more amped up and adrenaline would take over and I FELT more of like a max-effort guy. I don't think I was technically a max-effort – I'm not going to go up there and throw 100 miles an hour – but I felt like I threw harder and there was more effort being put into each single pitch, where as a starter you can't just go out there and – I mean, I can't, I guess – some guys can go out there and throw 100 miles an hour for seven innings, but I feel like if I go out in the first inning I can't just cash out and throw as hard as I can for the first few innings. I got to pace myself throughout the game.

On a day where you're starting, what's the routine like for you?

Just get to the field and do my normal stuff. I usually get in the hot tub, warm up a little bit, go get ready. About an hour before the game I go in and get a stretch from [Bob] Tarpey, the trainer, get stretched out, go back to the clubhouse, get my stuff, go out to the field and do my warmup. I don't really have a lot of crazy things I do. I don't eat any certain thing or do anything other than that. Really, my routine just starts about two hours before the game, two or three hours before the game, just get up here and do my normal thing, try to get my arm and my body stretched out and ready for the game, go out, do my long toss, and then get on the mound and warm up, go sit in the dugout and wait for my turn. That's pretty much it.

I know some guys, you don't talk to them, you don't look at them, you don't breathe near them when they're starting. Are you that intense?

No, I'm pretty laid back. I usually play around in the clubhouse on the stereo. I'll put my iPod on, play some music, and I talk and watch TV. It's not like I'm some zombie or somebody that you can't talk to or have to be scared of. I'm not like that. I don't take it that seriously. I mean, I take it serious, but I'm not that intense about it, I guess.

This year, you're throwing to a guy who is one of the top catching prospects in all of baseball, in Travis d'Arnaud. From a pitcher's perspective, what is it that makes Travis so good to throw to?

He's got really strong hands, or wrists. Especially for me, being a sinker ball guy, my ball's running down all the time, and a lot of times, with some catchers – not naming any names or anything – just some catchers, in receiving, have a tendency to go with the pitch, or they'll bring the ball down a little bit and you don't get a lot of low strikes. But he's got strong, strong hands and stays with the pitch and you get a lot of calls like that. He's a big guy, so he's an easy target to throw to. Calls a really good game, you know, he seems to know the ins and outs of each hitter, he reads the hitter and where they're standing in the box and as the game goes on he does a really good job of just having a game plan. The good thing about both of our catchers, him and Yan Gomes both, are very good about – I feel like when I'm throwing to them I feel like I don't have to think a whole lot, which is good for me. I don't need to be thinking too much [laughs]. They're a lot smarter than me, so it's good to throw to those guys. You know that they know what they're doing, they know what they're calling, so I trust when they put the fingers down that whatever they're thinking in their head, I'm like, "Okay, I trust you. I can throw that." So that's for sure a good thing to throw to. They both swing the bat pretty well too, so all-around, they're both great players.

So it sounds like there's a lot of respect that you have for them.

Oh yeah, for sure. The thing is, it's a team game, and we're all a team. But out there, a lot of times, it feels like it's me and whoever I'm throwing to that day, whether it be Yan or Travis. We're a team against the other guys, trying to get these guys out. So yeah, there is a lot of respect, especially for they're both young guys and they seem like they're way ahead of where they should be at this point in their careers.

When we had talked last year, you mentioned that you and Kyle Drabek were friends. Do you guys still keep in touch now that he's up in Toronto?

Oh yeah. We've been texting back and forth some and just keeping in touch with how he's doing and telling him, "Good job," here and there after his starts. Yeah, we still keep in touch.

I saw last night as I was putting these questions together that Eric Thames was just called up to Toronto. And obviously, that's a call that you want to get yourself, but how good does it feel when you hear about a former teammate getting that call?

It's awesome. Especially guys that you went to battle with the year before and guys that you get close to and you learn to love. This organization to me feels like a really close-knit group, and especially last year and this team this year, we've all gotten to be pretty close, not only as players but as friends off the field, and it's cool to see guys like him and [David] Cooper go to the big leagues, get up there and get their shot at it. That's really cool because it's what we all started playing this game to do and they get to realize their dream and it's pretty awesome.

Seems like a lot of the guys that I've talked to just this year are, like you said you are, like laid back, kind of relaxed. You take it seriously, but you're not killing yourself every day you're going out there.

Yeah, and I think that's the thing. I guess everybody's different, but it's not like any other sport where your season's 16 games, like football or anything. It's a long year. You're here every single day from the beginning of February until the end of September, depending on playoffs. It's a long season, it's a grind, and I think if you went out there and you were 100% effort every single day, I just feel like it'll lead to injuries or a mental institution, one of the two.

Stewart made his Major League debut with the Blue Jays on June 16. Six weeks later, he was traded at the July 31 deadline for the second time in his career, moving to the Chicago White Sox in exchange for Edwin Jackson and Mark Teahen. In 13 Major League games, 10 of them for the White Sox, he was 2-6 with a 5.88 ERA in 67 1/3 innings.

--Originally posted May 23, 2011 by Brian Moynahan

Kyle Weiland
Pawtucket Red Sox (Boston Red Sox)

Selected by the Boston Red Sox in the third round of the 2008 draft, Notre Dame product Kyle Weiland has been steadily making his way through the minor league system. The Red Sox have definitely taken their time to take this one-time reliever and turn him into a future starter. Weiland has pitched for every level in Boston's farm system, starting in Lowell in 2008 and moving his way up to Pawtucket for the 2011 campaign. The 6-foot-4 right-hander took some time after a recent start to talk about staying consistent.

When you pitched at Notre Dame you were a closer, and a successful one at that. When you were drafted by the Red Sox, however, they began to use you as a starter. What would you say is the biggest difference between the two and which would you prefer?

Well there's a big difference, when you come in as a reliever, especially a closer, you're feeding off of adrenaline. When the game is on the line, it's a great feeling, and it's a lot of fun pitching as a closer. As a starter, at least for me it's a lot more relaxed, you have to have a more balanced effort level in order to go deep into the games. You can't blow it all out in the first few innings. You also have to think through some situations, and make some adjustments in-game, as a reliever you don't have to do that...you just go out there and give it all you got.

When you first came into the league, you're curveball seemed to act more like a slurve*. During your last start you struck out four hitters with the curve, how has that developed since your days in Lowell (with the Spinners)?

I've just gotten more consistent, I'd say that slurve that you're calling it was maybe a few nights early on in my career was definitely not consistent, being the late biting curve ball that I try to get today or a slurve. It's hit or miss depending on the day, it's one thing that I've tried to be more consistent with and try to find the right mechanics to keep that consistency.

The second half of your season last year was kind of a rough stretch with Portland, then you start the year in Pawtucket. What you would say the biggest difference is between last year and this year being much more successful at a higher professional level?

It's got to be consistency. Finding a good routine between each five days is definitely key. It's more experience, throwing more innings, and the more innings you throw the better pitcher you are going to become and the more you're going to learn. I've also had the opportunity to pick the brains of all the veterans on the staff, guys like [Brandon] Duckworth, and [Kevin] Millwood, these guys have helped a tremendous amount of my development this year, so I got to credit them.

How important are guys like Duckworth, Millwood and even [Hideki] Okajima to have in the locker room as a young pitcher?

It's definitely an advantage. I wouldn't say it's necessary; you can still play a game without them. To have them here this year is something that I haven't experienced in the past, it's been a huge advantage for me. Just to watch them, how they go about pitching, and how they go about day to day work, even be able to talk to them about certain things.

Have you heard anything about a possible call up? Are you just taking things day by day and not letting yourself get caught up in that, just waiting for your time to come? Or do you look to see if there might be openings in the not so distant future?

Nah that's not something that you discuss with guys, when it happens you find out that day. That's not anything that we [Pawtucket] need to concern ourselves with, because it's out of

169

our control and when that day happens it happens and I have to be prepared for it.

Coming into the All-Star break what are you looking to achieve in the second half of the season? Are there major improvements that you feel you have to make going forward?

To continue to build on the start of the first half. I had a little bit of a dip a few starts ago where I lost some consistency with my fastball, but those things are always going to happen. Pretty much I want to build on what's been going on in the first half, stay consistent and try to be even more consistent, maybe throw more innings each outing.

When doing some research for the interview, Baseball America wrote about Weiland's curveball and referred to it as more of a slurve.

Weiland made his Major League debut on July 10. He was ejected in the fifth inning after hitting two batters. He was 0-3 in seven appearances for the Red Sox and 8-10, 3.58 in 24 starts for Pawtucket.

--Originally posted July 8, 2011 by Chris Fee

MiLB.com

Stetson Allie & Justin Meccage
State College Spikes (Pittsburgh Pirates)

Entering the 2011 season, Stetson Allie was one of the most intriguing players in the New York-Penn League. Pittsburgh's second-round pick in the 2010 Draft, he signed late and spent some time with the Spikes in late August, but did not see game action.

Allie was a logical choice for my first NYPL Notebook, which appeared on MiLB.com on July 1. In preparing for that story, I spoke with both Allie and his pitching coach, Justin Meccage, about his famously fast fastball, his secondary pitches, and the challenging transition from high school baseball to the professional ranks.

First thing I've got to ask you: your first name - where did that come from? Were you named for somebody or something?

You know what, I grew up in Orlando, Florida, and I want to say it was from the school Stetson down in Florida, but I'm not quite sure. Could be the hat, could be the cologne.

You made your professional debut pretty recently here, just within the last week, 10 days. What was that like stepping out on the field as a professional for the first time, getting ready to make your first start?

It was great. Had my family here, and friends. Was very anxious, can't wait for another start. I feel like I did alright for my first start but there's always room for improvement and I can't wait to get up on the mound again.

How did your second appearance compare to that first time out?

I thought my first one was better. Second one, I gave up one earned, one unearned, I think. But I had more walks, was missing

174

arm-side high again, and really been working on fixing that and it's been going well so far so I'm excited for the next start.

Talking about things that you were fixing – one of the things that was kind of noted about you was that you throw harder than hell but you had some trouble with your command when you're out there. Is there anything in particular that you've been working on, that you've changed or focused on to help improve that?

Yeah, I always tried to blow it by people, now I've started learning how to pitch. You don't have to throw in the upper-90s to get people out, you know, pitch to contact and work on my offspeed.

You still throw a fastball, slider, change? On a scale of like 1-10, how comfortable would you be with each of those pitches?

Fastball I'm very comfortable with. When I have been pitching I haven't been missing by much. Slider, probably very comfortable with. I feel like I'm an 8 or a 9 on that. And changeup, you know, it's still a work in progress, it has its days. I'd probably say a 5 or 6.

Are there any plans to add anything else to that, or is that what you're going with for now until you get comfortable?

Right now, yeah, it's fastball-change-slider.

You also mentioned not trying to throw the ball through a wall every time. Has it been tough to sort of adjust to that mindset where you have to take a little bit something off and work on hitting spots and saving your energy to get deeper into games?

Yeah, no doubt. They really wanted me to take some velocity off. Really just fastball command, pitching to contact, keep my pitch count down, and if I do get the opportunity, bury them with the slider.

When you're out there on the mound right now, in the middle of a game, what are you thinking about? What are you focusing on?

We've always talked about three pitches or less to contact. Definitely that keeps your pitch count down, keeps the defense in the game, on their toes.

Were you always able to throw hard? Is that something that's always been part of your game?

Yeah. I was originally a shortstop-third baseman, and always had a pretty good arm, and senior year I finally started pitching. It worked out well, ever since then I've been a pitcher and I really have enjoyed it.

I read a couple things, a couple places could see you playing third base. I thought that might be something at some point that if pitching didn't work out you could come back to, but obviously it's crazy early to be talking like that. Is that something you miss though, getting out there and swinging and playing every day?

No, not at all actually. I really just try to focus on pitching and getting to the next level, and focusing on that. It's not bad. I enjoy seeing hitters take BP and I don't even really miss it that much.

As far as transitioning from playing high school ball to the pros, what's been the easiest part of that transition?

The easiest part? I think people always said playing every day was the toughest. I've been fine with that. I enjoy learning new things, so that's been great.

176

What's been the hardest part of the transition?

I would say either throwing every day or pitching every fifth day. If you do bad, you've got five days to think about it. But I've really gotten good with that, and letting stuff go, and just focusing and getting mentally prepared for the next start.

You spent some time in State College last season, just kind of working out and observing. How did that benefit you to get out there and start your career this year?

Definitely. Got to see all the fans, under the lights, see some older guys pitch under the lights, and get used to throwing every day. All that stuff.

Was there any disappointment to start out the season this year in extended and then State College instead of going to West Virginia right away?

Oh no, not at all. I kind of expected it, you know, a first-year pitcher guy. I need to learn some stuff, definitely get my fastball command better. I wasn't disappointed at all. I know getting to the next level is a process and I'm willing to go through it right now.

I was looking through the Draft results from last year. Am I correct that one of your high school teammates [Alex Lavisky] plays for Mahoning Valley this year?

Yes, we actually played them today.

Yeah, I was going to ask you about that. I didn't know if you guys had connected at all over the last few days when your teams have been going against each other.

Yeah, we talked for a while before the games in Mahoning Valley. Good buddies, always competing against each other, but definitely good buddies.

177

Is it strange at all to have that distance now because you've gone from being teammates to being on opposite sides?

No, not at all. We didn't expect to go on the same team in the Draft. It's good to see his success and I'm sure he's happy about my success.

I read that you and Jameson Taillon had become close last year after the Draft. Do you guys still talk and communicate about things?

Yeah we always talk. We'll always be buddies. He's doing good and he always asks me how I'm doing. We've definitely built up a relationship.

One story I saw had you guys and Tony Sanchez as this trio of hot young prospects that could really impact the future of the Pirates. Is there any pressure that comes from that: as a 20-year-old kid, you're the savior?

I try to not even to really think about that. I just want to focus on doing my job here, getting better every day, and really just trying not to focus on the pressure of getting there. Just do my thing and everything will fall into place.

JUSTIN MECCAGE

I'm looking for the progression you've seen in [Stetson] this year, the stuff you guys have been working on, things like that.

I've had [Stetson] since spring training, but I had him in extended spring training, and then had him the full time since he's been here in State College, and seen some major progress in a lot of different areas. The biggest area would be the mental side of things, being able to handle certain situations both on and off the field. That's kind of what we attacked first, the pressures, the ability to throw strikes with his pitches, the ability to do the intangible things like fielding bunts and fielding his position, covering first base, all that kind of stuff. Just recently we've started to attack the delivery a little bit, the mechanics of pitching, so I think his mental side is so much better from when we started. And now that he's mentally in pretty good shape we feel like we can attack the physical side of things with the delivery, and that's what we've been doing here as of recent.

I asked him the easiest thing and the hardest thing to deal with and he said one of the harder things was when you're starting, you go out and have a bad outing, you've got five days to think about it.

That's the other thing we've tried to educate him on is the process of the five days and how important those five days are on improving and building on some of the things that you need to work on. The mental side is part of that too, understanding what you did well and understanding what you didn't do well in the previous outing, and working that, attacking that. And then the rehab side of things, the recovery process, the conditioning part, taking care of the arm, and just getting used to that, whereas in high school he probably threw a day and then maybe two days later was back on the bump. Or he was in a position, so there wasn't a whole lot of time to think, there wasn't a whole lot of time for anything but playing. So that's the other side of things that we've tackled.

So on the physical side of things, he had also said that he had taken a lot of the heat out of his fastball for right now. Trying to work on his command more, that's a big focus for you guys?

Yes, that's what we're trying to do. Stetson's got a very nice arm, he's very talented, he could throw 100 miles an hour if he wanted. I'm not sure if he'd know where it was going, so we try to keep him somewhere at about 90% velocity, somewhere between 92-95 [miles per hour] with command of the pitch, and

179

understanding that you can go to that 100% in certain counts and certain situations. But early in the counts and things like that, using that 90% fastball, and being able to command that is something you have to learn, so that's what we're going through. If he's going to pitch in the big leagues, that's something that he's going to need to grasp, so we've attacked it that way.

So is that the sort of thing that you look at like, he learns it now, he straightens out and learns to pitch at that level now – over time, will he be able to throw harder more consistently, or is this where he's aiming for long-term success?

No, I think it's a process. Down the road, it might be more velocity as he gets physically stronger, as he goes through some of that stuff. But on our side, there's nothing wrong with a 92-96 located fastball. It's a lot easier to locate when you're under control and doing some of those things, whereas if you're trying to throw a hundred it's very difficult to locate. And the other part of that is lasting, health-wise. If you're always throwing with max effort, breakdowns happen and some of those things happen a lot more frequent than if you're nice and easy. We call it "easy gas." Free and easy in the delivery, whereas when the effort level is high, injuries and things like that become more and more of a possibility. So there'll be times, like I said, in certain situations, that he might need that extra little bit. And he knows that it's in there and that's what we've got to get him to understand.

How have his secondary pitches been?

Very good. Well, potentially they're very good. Inconsistent. Part of that is overthrowing them sometimes. When he's right, his slider is very good. It's in the upper 80s, maybe even touching 90, with real good depth, and late depth. It's a strikeout pitch. And at times you see command out of it, when he's not trying to overthrow it. And then the changeup's really developed, and that's something that we worked real hard on over the last three months, is the changeup development and throwing program and

180

things like that, so that can become a useable pitch in games, and there are times that it's very useable. As far as the physical side of things, the changeup development has probably been the biggest improvement of anything. It's an upper 80s changeup, maybe a little bit firm at times, but it's got late down sink to it, which is something you look for, as long as there's arm speed. The secondary stuff is there, it's just the consistency of the secondary stuff, which is the issue with all of these pitchers. It's not just Stetson Allie, it's that the 18-, 19-, 20-year-old pitcher is trying to figure out that secondary command and that's something that he's going through too.

It's easy to forget that sometimes, that just because a kid has a big name and a big arm doesn't make him any different.

That's right. Some of the same problems he has, 90% of these other guys have too. He's just extremely talented, so he sticks out a little bit more.

Allie finished his first professional season 0-2 with a 6.58 ERA in 15 games, including seven starts. He struck out 28 batters and walked 29 in 26 innings.

--Brian Moynahan

Aaron Altherr & Mickey Morandini
Williamsport Crosscutters (Philadelphia Phillies)

One of Philadelphia's top prospects, Altherr began the season in Low-A Lakewood, where he got off to a rough start in his first 41 games. He was assigned to Williamsport when the New York-Penn League season started in mid-June.

Altherr was the subject of my second NYPL Notebook, which appeared on MiLB.com on July 8. I spoke with him and his manager, Mickey Morandini, about spending a second season with the Crosscutters, his reaction when he learned of the move, and what he needed to do to begin moving back up the system.

Coming out of the spring, was the plan for you to spend the entire season in Lakewood?

Yeah, that was the plan, but just from my struggles they wanted me to come down here, get my confidence back. I'm hoping to get right back up there. Just keep on playing good and hopefully they'll send me right back up.

When did you find out that you were going to be going back down to Williamsport? I know it was a little bit before the season started.

It was about a week before the Williamsport season started. They told me and then I sat out for a few games in Lakewood before I came to Williamsport.

What was your reaction when they told you that you were going to be headed back to Williamsport?

At first I was a little disappointed, but I realized what they were trying to do. It was all for the best, it really is. I've just got to perform and start doing well and get my confidence back up, which, I've gotten it back up there. Now I'm fine with it. Just ready to play every day and have fun doing it.

Those first couple months, where were you at mentally? Was it just that it started out as a little slump and then just kept getting more frustrating?

Yeah, I had a real slow start, and it was just tough for me to break out of that slump, mentally. I think that was another reason for me to come down here was to clear my mind, get a fresh new start, and that's all I think it was, really.

Did it help that it was kind of a familiar place too, where you'd played there last year?

Definitely. Definitely helps.

Is there anything mechanically with your swing that you tried to tinker with when you came down, to see if that would help?

Basically I went right back to what I was doing in Spring Training. In Spring Training I was hitting the cover off the ball, I was hitting it real good, and I kind of got away from it during the season in Lakewood. So I had to get right back to where I was in Spring Training and I feel like I've done that.

Did they give you any sort of a heads-up, like a goal to shoot for, as in, "Hey, if you reach this, we may be looking to bring you back up there"?

No, they didn't give me any goals. Just told me to play well and I've got a great shot of going right back up to Lakewood.

How has your time been in Williamsport this year? How have you felt about it?

183

I feel great. I'm real comfortable here. I feel like there's no pressure on me down here as much as there was in Lakewood. I feel like I can just come out here and play my game and not worry about anything. At first I thought it was going to be a bad thing, but it's really turned out to be great.

So it sounds like the challenge is just going to be carrying those positive feelings back up with you when you go up. You know, taking that positive mindset back up?

Right, yeah, definitely that. Just keep that mindset that I'll hopefully be back up there and keep hitting the ball hard.

Last year you started off in the Gulf Coast League again after playing there the year before. Does this feel at all similar to that, running through a league again and getting a second shot at it, a second chance to prove yourself more?

It's a similar situation, because last year I was also down on myself at first for being stuck in the GCL again. Started off slow, then I just ended up clearing my head, started playing ball the way I know I can, and that's when things started picking up for me. And again, just like last year, it was the greatest thing that could've happened to me, just to stay down in the GCL, get my swing right, and work my way up, which I did. And I did well up here too. It's all for the good, I think, everything that happens.

Everybody's different, right?

Yeah. Everybody's got a different path.

MICKEY MORANDINI

I just talked to Aaron and I'm trying to flesh it out now with the coaching perspective on what you've seen from him this season and where he's come from, from when he first got there to now.

184

This is really the first time I've seen him consistently, so I've seen him for 18 games here, but he's been one of our most consistent hitters, he's hitting over .300, he's played an outstanding leftfield for us. He's made several running and diving catches in left-centerfield for us. The guy can do it all. He can lay down a bunt, he's got some speed, he's stolen some bases for us. He's hit a couple homeruns, and I expect that as he gets a little more mature and a little stronger that he's going to be hitting more homeruns than he is now. He's done a great job for us.

When he and I talked, we talked a little bit about his rough start this season in Lakewood. Is there anything mechanically he worked on when he got to Williamsport? Was there anything that he worked on to try to right the ship?

We haven't really changed too much with him because like I said, when he was in Lakewood we hadn't seen him too much. I mean, he came here and got off to a pretty hot start for us. He's been pretty consistent, so we really haven't changed much with him. I think the key for him is just swinging down on the ball. He's a big kid, so just swinging down on the ball and making contact. I tell you, when he makes contact he can hit the ball a long way. He's an alley, doubles kind of hitter right now, and like I said, he can use his speed a little bit.

But we haven't changed too much with him because he's hitting the ball good. I think he's hitting .325 or something like that. You're hitting the ball like that, there's not too much we can do mechanically that needs to change right now.

From his perspective it sounded like confidence was the thing he struggled with and was trying to maintain a high level.

Yeah, and I think that's typical of a young player. You want to get off to that good start and when you don't you start to press a little bit, and obviously when you're pressing you're not going to do the things you're capable of doing. But he came in here, like I said, he got off to a pretty good start right away and I think that relaxed him a little bit, and he's carried that on through the first eighteen games.

I understand you haven't seen a lot of him. It's definitely good to hear what you have seen. That's what I was looking for, kind of where he's at.

We've been very happy. He goes about his business, works hard. He's a quiet kid, goes about his business, does what he has to do. He's willing to listen, and that's part of the battle when you're a young kid, is being able to listen and make adjustments. He's done a great job.

Altherr cooled off some after a hot start in Williamsport, but still ended the season with a .260 average, five homeruns, 31 RBI, and 25 steals in 71 games.

--Brian Moynahan

Garin Cecchini & Rich Gedman
Lowell Spinners (Boston Red Sox)

The subject of the New York-Penn League Notebook for July 22 was Garin Cecchini, Boston's fourth round pick in the 2010 Draft. A potential first-rounder, Cecchini's stock slipped when he tore his ACL early in his senior year of high school. Because of the injury, his professional debut was delayed until this season, when he started off with the Lowell Spinners in mid-June.

I caught up with Garin last week, the second of three straight interviews he did before a game against the Vermont Lake Monsters. (When Lowell's Director of Media Relations, Jon Boswell, brought him over, I asked Cecchini if he talked all the time or if he actually played baseball; he appears to be constantly in demand.) We spoke about the state of his knee, his approach at the plate, and his early success as a base stealer.

First things first, how's the knee doing?

Knee's doing perfect, man, it's 100% now. It's a blessing because I had tendonitis bad last year and I was like, "Ooh, is it torn? Is it torn?" No, it's not torn, you know, kept telling the doctors, "No it's not torn, no it's not torn." It was just tendonitis and I'm glad that tendonitis is gone and my leg strengthened, and I'm glad that I'm here.

So that was after your original injury, they were concerned that you had something else going on?

Well no, I was concerned. I thought, "Shoot it's re-torn, shoot it's re-torn." No, it's tendonitis. And they said tendonitis was going to happen. But now it's all gone so I'm glad I'm here.

Was it just your ACL that was involved or were there other ligaments in there too?

It was just my ACL, thank goodness, just my ACL.

That was early in the season, right?

Yeah, it was the ninth game of my high school season, 2010. We had 47 games scheduled that year, so I didn't even get through 25% of it.

Did you stick around with the team?

Oh yeah, yeah. I tore my ACL on a Thursday, I had surgery the next Thursday, and I was there Thursday night.

So within a week you were right back in the swing of things.

Yeah, right back, trying to cheer on my team to a state championship.

How'd they do?

They were semi-finalists. You know, we came up short, but it was a great year.

You didn't play at all last year, after the injury. When you finally got on the field this year, how did that feel?

It feels good. I'm glad to be in this great city of Lowell, right next to Boston. You get great fans, great field, great coaches, great organization, so it's great. I'm with the Red Sox, one of the best organizations in baseball – I feel like the best organization in baseball – so I'm glad I'm here.

In terms of your development, it's early obviously, just been a few weeks, but how do you feel you're progressing so far?

From the start of Spring Training to here, I've progressed a lot more than I thought I would. I'm getting better defensively, even though the errors are there, still getting better defensively. It's going to be a process – never played third [base] in my life. The at-bats...the stats say whatever they say, but I'm having quality at-bats and that's what matters. Hitting balls hard, go deep into counts, and like I said, I'm glad I'm here and I'm glad I'm starting my career in Lowell.

You mentioned the adjustment to third base. What's been the difficult part of that? You were a shortstop in high school?

Yeah, I was a shortstop. The toughest [adjustment] is the angles. Stuff comes much quicker there, you have much more time at short, you're back more. It's just different, man. But it's going to come, it's going to take time. I've only played there for five months. So once I get deeper in my career, years from now, it's going to get much better.

You've got hits in eight of your last 10 games, and you're starting to show a little power also. At the plate, how are you feeling different now than you were the first few weeks of the season and from extended [Spring Training] on?

I had a great extended spring, and then when I came here I felt like I had good quality at-bats – I was just jumping at the ball a little bit. The game was speeding up. A 90 mile an hour fastball was looking like 110. Now, [I'm] slowing stuff down, slowing my hands down, seeing the ball, and just hitting it, because I have to trust my swing. I feel like my swing's good enough, don't think about anything but seeing the ball and hitting the ball. That's what I'm doing right now and it's working out. So just trying to slow the game down, don't let it speed up on me.

So just a matter of getting the game speed repetition in.

Yeah, yeah. I mean, I don't even have 100 at-bats yet. I think I have 98 *[Ed. Note: he did]* or something like that. A hundred at-bats into the season, and I felt like it was a great first 100 at-bats. Even though they don't show whatever they don't show, I felt like the last 50 were a great 50 at-bats. So if we can keep that going, then everything's going to work out for itself.

It is interesting too, I've talked to up with the Blue Jays team in Manchester, in New Hampshire, and they mention the same thing: you can look at the stats all you want, but sometimes it's how you're feeling and how you're seeing things.

How you're seeing things, and what we're focused on here is developing quality at-bats. Adrian Gonzalez talks about it. Don't worry about the result, worry about having professional at-bats, and that's what I'm worried about. Swinging at a ball on top of your head, that's not a professional at-bat. Seeing the ball, laying off those curveballs in the dirt, laying off the changeups in the dirt, getting a good pitch, putting a good swing on it, wherever it goes, it goes. It's in someone else's hands.

I've read that you've drawn some pretty good reviews for your approach at the plate. I think I've seen it called an advanced approach. So it sounds like that's kind of what you're talking about, just kind of being patient.

Being patient, having an advanced approach and seeing the ball and putting a swing on a ball that you can hit. Swinging at a ball outside your zone or a good pitcher's pitch – unless you have two strikes – it's not a good pitch to hit.

We talked about the approach, we've heard about your swing a little bit, and your power potential, but 10 steals in 11 attempts – that's kind of snuck up on me, because everything I read said that you weren't going to be a stolen base guy. So what's going on with those? Is it just opportunity?

It is that, but – I don't know how to put this – I feel like I can pay attention to details a lot with pitchers. I know their timing. Pitchers are creatures of habit. If they're going to hold two seconds twice, they're probably going to hold it a third time. If they pick up, you steal. If they don't, you don't go. It's opportunity and being smart. Stealing bases is not just about speed. It's not just about speed at all. It's about getting good jumps, reading pitchers, seeing what their tendencies are, knowing when to go – that's what base stealing is. So I feel like I'm good at that and that's why I have 10 stolen bags.

So you've picked that up pretty quick, because we're not very far into the season here.

Right, yeah. You try to. You're in the dugout and you see everyone else on base and you see what the pitcher's doing. How many times is he going to look to second? If he's going to look twice four times in a row, he's probably going to look twice the fifth time in a row, you know what I mean? So…go. After he looks twice, just go. It's just picking up on tendencies.

RICH GEDMAN

I talked to Garin a bit about his development and I'd just kind of like to get the coaching perspective on where he's at, how far he's come, things like that.

He's diligent about the way he goes about his business in the cage. He has a very good approach to hitting. I would say that it's a middle to the other way approach, stays inside the ball very well. When they get him out of his approach sometimes, he rolls it over some, but for the most part he's been pretty good about staying with what he believes in. I think it's a great way to start into pro ball, staying on the ball, trusting your swing. It produces a lot of line drives the other way, it helps you stay on the breaking ball.

So all in all, I think in the time I've seen him since spring training, he's been very consistent with his approach. And in some ways he hasn't got the results that he probably should have, in terms of numbers. But as long as he continues with that approach, he's going to develop, he's going to learn how to pull the ball. And I hope he doesn't try to force it too soon. I think sometimes when you play with some older kids who may be a little bigger and a little stronger, maybe hit some homeruns, you feel some pressure to feel like you have to match them. He doesn't. He has a good approach to hitting. Plays the ball through the middle of the field, stays behind the ball very well, and the more pitching he sees, both left and right, the better he's going to get. He has limited experience but high-end tools. Especially at the plate.

Yeah, we talked a little bit about patience. He talked about the importance of a patient approach at the plate, so it sounds like what you're saying is that you want him to just be patient all the way around and don't try to do more than he's ready to do right now.

I have this little saying: "What you have is good enough." And sometimes you can try to accelerate that. You recognize that, well, the ball inside is giving me a little bit of trouble. Well, I'm betting that 70-80% of the balls pitched are designed to be away. So why wouldn't I stay with something that's going to be strong in its approach rather than go for something where I'm going to look in and try to go for power? To me it doesn't make any sense. I think he's got a good swing, he needs to stay with that swing and as he gets bigger, strong, more experienced, he'll gain greater knowledge of the strike zone plus also be able to do more pick and select and choose times to be a little more aggressive.

The day after this story ran at MiLB.com, Cecchini was hit by a pitch, breaking his wrist and sidelining him for the rest of the season. He finished his professional debut with a .298 batting average, three homeruns, 23 RBI, and 12 stolen bases in 32 games.

--Originally posted July 26, 2011 by Brian Moynahan

Alexander Colome
Charlotte Stone Crabs (Tampa Bay Rays)

This interview was done for MiLB.com on April 28 while Colome was pitching for the Port Charlotte Stone Crabs of the Florida State League. Colome's answers were translated by fellow Stone Crab Alex Koronas.

So how would you describe your season so far?

He said it's been going well. He has had two that were not so great, two that were so-so, and one that was really good, so he feels he is getting stronger and getting better.

What are you trying to improve on this season, both as a person and as a ballplayer?

He is working on locating his pitches down in the zone. He's got the stuff, he now has to learn where to throw it.

What are your personal goals for the season?

To do what he knows he has to do. To do what he is capable of doing and having a great season.

You pitched very well at home so far. What is it about pitching at Port Charlotte that brings out the best in you? And what do you have to do to pitch on the road just as well?

He says he feels comfortable pitching here at home, but there is really no difference between pitching at home or on the road for him. The days he pitched at home he was locating better and throwing his pitches a lot better. He says you always feel better when you are pitching at home because you get the support.

193

Your uncle Jesus pitched in the majors. Do you talk to him often, and what advice has he given you on being a better pitcher?

They talk all the time. They talk baseball in general, pitching, what pitch to throw, and how to react on the field. You know, just baseball talk.

You've struck out a lot of batters in your career. How important is getting strikeouts?

Striking out people is a good feeling and it's something he has always done and it makes him feel good and it is part of his game.

Colome played for the Stone Crabs until mid-July, compiling a 9-5 record and 3.66 ERA. Following a promotion to Double-A Montgomery, he was 3-4 with a 4.15 ERA.

--Mike Lortz

Cito Culver

Staten Island Yankees (New York Yankees)

The original plan called for me to write about Culver early on in the summer, but we were unable to get together for an interview. I had to wait until Staten Island came to Lowell to speak with him, which worked out for the best as he ended up being the last Notebook subject of the season.

Last year in the Prospect Handbook, Baseball America said that a lot of people in the industry were surprised last year when the Yankees drafted you in the first round. Obviously you're a top talent, number three in the state of New York. Was it at all surprising to you when you got the call that they were looking to pick you up that early?

I knew that they were interested, but I didn't know it was to first-round level. I knew they were really interested, they came to a lot of my high school games, but I didn't know that was going to happen until the day of the Draft.

So did they call you up before they took you and say, "Hey..." How did that happen?

They called me up and said they were thinking about taking me, and just left it at that. And then I got a call later that night, like five minutes before their pick, to tell me that I was going to be their number one.

What's your reaction like when you hear something like that?

Coming from New York, I've been a diehard Yankee fan my whole life. All I ever wanted to do is play shortstop for the New York Yankees, so it was a once-in-a-lifetime moment for me.

You mention playing shortstop for the Yankees. For an outsider, a fan or whatever, being drafted as a shortstop by

195

the Yankees seems like it's got to be one of the most pressure-filled just because of who plays shortstop now for the Yankees. Does any of that "Derek Jeter's replacement" pressure come down to you, or are you still far enough removed from it that it doesn't really bother you?

I never really look at it as "replacing" him, because who can replace an all-time great? Do I look forward to playing that position once he's finished with baseball? Yeah [laughs]. But the Yankees do a really good job of keeping the pressure off me, just letting me play and not pressuring me, not pushing me too fast. I've got all the time in the world, really, so it's been fun. I haven't really looked at it like that.

How often do people ask you about Derek Jeter?

A lot, a lot, a lot. They wonder if I've met him, or if I talk to him and stuff like that. Just a lot.

You mentioned not getting pressured, not getting rushed at all. You signed really quickly after the Draft last year and you got a couple hundred at-bats between the GCL and Staten Island. How did that benefit you to jump right in the swing of it, right from high school to the pros?

I think I benefitted from it a lot, just getting used to the everyday grind and just the routine of a professional ballplayer. It takes a lot to get used to and I think that helped me out a lot, signing fast. I just wanted to play, too. I was just going to be sitting at home anyway, so I might as well.

Was there any disappointment in regards to coming back to Staten Island to stay the full year this year? Were you expecting anything more of yourself or was it kind of the expectation that you were going to be here for the season this year even though you spent some time here last year?

196

I have no control over that. All I have control over is my effort and my play, and that's all I do. Wherever they put me is where they think is the best fit, and they've been doing this for a lot of years. I have faith in them.

Is there any specific area where you feel like you've improved this year?

I think from last year, my entire game has improved. Defensively, offensively. I still have a lot more to improve, in all facets of the game. Just trying to learn as I go, really.

Something jumped out at me from looking at your stats. There's a pretty big disparity between your home and your road stats. You hit really well on the road and your batting average is a lot lower at home. Is that just something that, it is what it is, or is there any particular cause for it?

I don't know. I'm wondering the same thing. I don't know, man, it's just something that happened, really. It could easily be the other way around. It doesn't really...I don't know.

And then also along those lines, since the All-Star break you've been in a little bit of a slump. Again, is there a cause for that? Is it just that it's late in the season, you're trying to bust through that wall, or is it just one of those things you go through?

I just think as a baseball player you're going to go through slumps. You don't really have control over when they come, and just try to fight through it, take it an at-bat at a time and try not to get too down on myself, because I have high expectations for myself, and that can sometimes hurt you as a ballplayer. So I just try to stay even-keel for the most part and just try to do what I can control, and that's play good defense. I can't control the results at the plate. Just have good at-bats and go from there.

I personally like it when a guy gets a chance to go back to his hometown or home area and play ball. You got that chance earlier this year when you went back to Batavia. What was it like to be able to go home and play in front of family and friends?

It was really exciting. I actually felt really comfortable in that situation, all my friends and all my family just there to support me, and it was a really good turnout. I enjoyed it a lot.

You didn't disappoint them either, with a couple homers in that first game.

I just thank God for that because I don't know where that came from, but it felt good. It felt really good.

In his second professional season, Culver hit .250 with two homeruns and 33 RBI. He also stole 10 bases without being caught and helped the Staten Island Yankees to the sixth New York-Penn League championship in team history.

--Brian Moynahan

Jarek Cunningham
Bradenton Marauders (Pittsburgh Pirates)

This interview was done while on assignment for MiLB.com on May 21. Cunningham at the time was among the Florida State League leaders in slugging and extra base hits.

You are hitting the ball really well so far this year. You are getting a large number of extra-base hits already this season. Are you trying to drive the ball more than in years past?

Not really trying to. I'm just widening the base a little bit in my swing, make solid contact, and put the ball in play more.

I read an interesting stat. Did you know you are hitting over .500 with more than half your home runs in the seventh inning? Is there something about the seventh inning stretch that invigorates you?

I don't know. Maybe I am just getting comfortable in the game.

Are any of your power numbers attributable to strength and conditioning? I saw you put some weight on since your high school days.

Yeah, this offseason was big. I worked out all offseason in Arizona and I definitely think that contributed.

Anything specific you worked on out there?

I did a lot more weights than normal. I usually just do band work and a little weights but this year I did mostly weights.

Speaking of years past, you were a 12th round pick, right?

18th.

Sorry. You were an 18th round pick out of high school and you went pro. You didn't do the college route. What was the decision process there?

It was one of those things where I had the opportunity to do something I've wanted to do since I was a kid.

You missed your senior year of high school with an ACL injury and then missed the whole season again with an ACL injury in 2009, how are things today?

They are good. I don't feel a thing anymore in my knee. I am braceless and everything is strong.

Can you talk a bit about your rehab in '09 and how it has made you the player you are today?

Missing a season, especially after I played a year in the GCL (Gulf Coast League), it's one of those things where you watch every day and it makes you want to work that much more and work that much harder to get back to where you know you can be.

Last year you struggled a bit towards the end of the season. What lessons did you take from that experience into this year?

Just my work before games. Especially down here, with how hot it is, you really have to be conscious of how much work you put in before so you still have it for the games.

When you say the amount of work, what do you mean?

The amount of groundballs you take, the amount of swings. Controlling what I do in the weight room before. It's more maintenance.

You've played second, short, and third in your career. What's your preference on positions?

I think now second because I played the whole season there last year and played there so far this year. I think it would be tough to back to the other side of the diamond. It would another transition phase for me.

And finally, what are your goals for this year? Any team or personal goals?

Personally, it's to stay consistent. Last year I fell off, but this year I want to carry it all the way through. And as a team, we need to put it all together. We have a great team, but we just can't put it all together on both sides of the ball on the same day.

Sorry, one more last thing. I saw you guys also the other day in an 11-10 game. In the sixth or seventh inning, you bunted. Was that your call or was that someone else? Everyone was jacking the ball all over the field that whole game, and I was really surprised you tried to lay one down especially with your power numbers.

That was the manager's call. That was one thing they taught me early in the season to be able to do. So I have that at the next level.

So that is something that you are conscious of, trying to lay one down?

Yeah, especially in the two hole, he wants me to be able to have that under my belt.

Cunningham was a Florida State League All-Star in 2011. He ended the season with 15 home runs, 23 doubles, and a .516 slugging percentage despite missing a large part of the second half with concussion symptoms.

--Mike Lortz

Matt Hobgood & Scott McGregor
Aberdeen IronBirds (Baltimore Orioles)

The New York-Penn League Notebook for August 5 featured Matt Hobgood of the Aberdeen IronBirds. Hobgood, the fifth overall pick in the 2009 Draft, struggled this season while rehabbing a strained rotator cuff. I was impressed, though, by his positive outlook and what appears to be a genuine good nature.

Matt and I spoke when the IronBirds visited Lowell last week. It was raining heavily and we were standing under the stands, which are very leaky. His glove got a little wet. I felt bad. Then we realized that if we moved three feet to the left, there were no leaks. Victory!

Anyway, we covered a number of topics, including the current state of Matt's velocity, how his injury affected him more than he realized at the time, and his ability to put bad outings behind him. After the rain stopped, I talked with his pitching coach, Scott McGregor, about where Matt is at right now.

How's your shoulder feeling at this point?

Feels good. It feels strong. My velocity is not all the way back to where it was. I think last outing Scotty McGregor, my pitching coach, said I was 88-91, basically. I hit 92 a couple times. I hit 93 once, which is what I've been doing, typically, each time out. Maybe hitting 93, hitting 92 a couple times.

It feels good. I'm trying to get my feel back for everything. I've always been somebody who's been used to going after hitters, throwing strikes and really attacking the zone, and now I'm trying to do that and it's hard because basically I stopped throwing last year in September, started throwing in December, found out about my arm – strained shoulder – stopped throwing (I threw like 30 pitches in December), and then rehabbed starting in January to the end of March. So I basically took off from September to March and didn't throw a ball.

So as you're throwing and then you're getting into pitching after not pitching for a while – my first game was on June 20 – it takes a while.

It's like your body forgets, almost.

Exactly. It is. My mechanics have changed a little bit, but my arm feels good and I think probably by next year my velocity will return to something similar like it was before.

It was a strained rotator cuff, right? Before you were officially diagnosed with that, how did that affect you? What were you feeling that kind of said, "Something's not right"?

When I came into camp in February 2010, I ended up breaking with Delmarva, but when I came in I just kind of felt okay. I know there's some speculation about my weight a little bit, but I didn't really think that would have a giant effect on my arm.

I came in and that whole year I was basically 87-90, maybe 87-91 some games, but as time went on I'd be 87-88, 87-89, and just kind of stayed there. Nothing higher, nothing lower. And my arm slot had dropped a little bit, from where in high school it was more a high three-quarter slot to where basically the whole season I was almost down to a low three-quarter. Not sidearm, but not three-quarters.

Was that compensating?

Yeah, I was. I didn't think I was, but in time, looking at video in high school and video in Delmarva, I realized. I kind of thought maybe it was my weight, but in going back I think it was just kind of…I couldn't pick out a particular time of when it got hurt.

Just over time, you noticed it? Your velocity was down, your arm slot dropped?

Yeah. It was kind of disappointing.

I call it kind of "baseball injured". You know, arm, shoulder, elbow. Had you ever had an injury like that before?

I've never been injured. Knock on wood, I've never had an elbow [injury]. I've had soreness. I've never had something where I've had to miss time. So the rehab process, missing time, it was all kind of new to me. It was a little frustrating. It still is kind of frustrating now, coming back, not having my velocity. But I feel like it is helping me as a pitcher. One thing I've been really happy with is my ground ball rate. Last year I think I was a 2.5, maybe, or something like that, and this year I've gotten hit around, but I think it's still at a 4.3 or something like that. When I get the ball down I get good movement and induce a lot of ground balls.

In terms of your repertoire, what pitches are you throwing right now?

Four-seam, two-seam, curveball, and I'm trying to work on a changeup. Changeup's something I probably need to work on the most, that's the pitch that's going to help me out I think once I get to High-A, Double-A. And I think the better the hitter where he's able to handle 93-94, if you can throw a changeup in any count, whenever you want, it's going to be that much more effective and keep the hitter going north-south, rather than a curveball which they can kind of sit on.

You mentioned getting hit around a little bit. The last couple times out you struggled. Is there a reason you can point to where you go, "Okay, THIS is why this is happening," or is that something where day-by-day you're trying to look at different things and figure out what's going on?

Each time out I want to go out and throw – they told me they want me to keep it roughly to four innings every time out, and I just want to go out and throw four scoreless if I can. I think the last two outings I've given up 15 or 16 runs or something. You know, I'm rehabbing, I'm coming back. I think it'd be different if I was going out with my best stuff, felt good and I was just getting hit around. Then maybe I'd be a little more concerned.

I know there's a lot of stuff I need to work on. I think last night, I felt like I caught some bad breaks. I had a lot of ground ball hits, a lot of singles that just didn't end up going to anybody, couple balls chopped over the infield, threw a passed ball that scored a run, so I didn't feel I pitched bad. Certainly I didn't pitch good but it was kind of just one of those games where everything's bad.

I know when I have a bad day or I'm not feeling good, work is the last place I want to be. When you have a few rough days or you're not feeling good, is it ever tough to go to the ballpark and put your work in? You seem like you're a pretty happy, upbeat guy.

Yeah, I am. It's funny because I go on my Twitter account, Facebook, whatever, I like to mess around and stuff. I think sometimes maybe people see that as me not taking it serious. I see it as turning the page. You know, I'm not going to sit there and dwell on it. If I go seven scoreless and give up two hits and lose, or if I go 2 2/3 innings and give up nine runs, I need to realize what I did wrong and move on. I'm not going to sit there and cry about it.

It's a new day.

Yeah, exactly, it's a new day. I'm not going to get all upset because my ERA went up or whatever. I think obviously as you get higher and higher you worry about those things, but I want to try to stay as even-keeled as I can, and I honestly am. I think I've learned that if you get all upset about stuff you'll take it into the next day, you'll take it into your bullpen, you'll take it into other facets of your game and it'll hurt you in the end, I think. So I try and turn the page every day.

205

When you were first injured, without really realizing it you noticed your velocity was down. Can you explain what it's like when you can't get your body and your arm to do the things you feel like they should be able to do?

Just frustration. I mean, that's about all I can say about it. Like I said, I've never had any arm problems. I've always been somebody who's been able to throw strikes. I think that was one of the reasons why I was so successful in high school. I enjoy going after people. I don't shy away from anybody. It's just frustration. There's nothing you can do about it. You got to take your licks. But I think next year will be a big year for me. Definitely going to focus on getting my weight back down a little bit to where it was in high school. My goal this offseason is to get under 240. I'll be working out in Arizona at API in Tempe. Like I said, there's a lot of things I need to work on. I'll be 21 tomorrow. Twenty-one's still pretty young, considering last year was only my first full season. I think I still have a lot of time.

Do you feel like sometimes people – commentators, fans – do you feel like they forget that you're only 20-, 21-years-old?

Yeah, I get it. I think there's a lot of organizations out there that are struggling, and I think the fans that have been around for a while, they want to see their team's win and I get that. I take pretty much everything with a grain of salt. I don't really listen to what other people say, but it's kind of like, hey, I am 20, going to be 21. Not everybody does go up, not everybody has the quick ascension, not everybody gets it right away, especially out of high school. I think if I was out of college, 21-22, I think I might've had a little more figured out, but I'm just trying to get better each day.

So are you here for the rest of the year?

I'll probably finish out the year here, yeah. I think that's their game plan.

206

You kind of addressed it already, but the path your development has taken – do you feel comfortable with it right now? Like you said, everybody's got their own path. Do you feel good about where you're at right now?

I wouldn't say good, but I'm not stressing. Like I said, I can honestly say that. I know a lot of people would probably rather me be in [High-A] Frederick on my way to Double-A. But like I said, that's not going to happen [this season]. I know in my heart that it will happen eventually, Lord willing that I can stay healthy and get back to where I need to be physically with my arm and my body. But sometimes good things take time. Rome's not built in a day and I'm trying to do the best I can. If I could I'd go out and fix my arm so I could throw 95 again but I can't do that. I have to do rehab, I have to get back and when you take 5-6 months off after throwing consistently with summer ball and high school and you're used to doing everything for a good period of time in a row...ask a hitter. Unless you're Josh Hamilton, take six months off from hitting and see what happens when you come back. It will take you a while to get back into a consistent groove of where you can really do well at your craft.

SCOTT McGREGOR

I'm looking for the coaching perspective on where Matt is at right now.

Right now he's just trying to make sure he stays healthy, and getting him back on the mound, getting his pitches in. Yesterday's line was not good, but I thought he threw the ball the best I've seen him throw in a while. It's a process for him right now and we just want to get him through this year. So I think that's our whole philosophy, just make sure he gets through and gets ready for next year, and hopefully next year he'll be back to where he was last year when he got hurt. He's working hard at it. Whenever you have the shoulder stuff, you develop some bad habits. You've just got to break some of those down right now.

Seems like he has a good attitude about things, though, as far as putting tough outings behind him.

A couple of the outings have been rough for him here, but he's maintained his composure out there and kept pitching and actually made pretty good pitches in situations. I give him credit for that. He's handled it well and as long as he keeps that up he'll be fine.

You're expecting to have him here the rest of the year?

Well, yeah. I know they were possibly trying to get him to go up to [Low-A] Delmarva, but the main thing is right now is to go out there every fifth day and stay healthy and just make improvements each time. That's what we're looking for.

And get back in the routine of actually pitching. He mentioned not throwing a ball for so long, it's like you forget.

Yeah, he's just working on some mechanical things right now, and once he gets those ironed out he can get back to pitching.

Hobgood made eight appearances for Aberdeen, including seven starts. He finished the season 0-6 with a 10.46 ERA, striking out 13 batters and walking 23.

--Originally posted August 9, 2011 by Brian Moynahan

Kyle Jensen
Jupiter Hammerheads (Florida Marlins)

This interview was conducted on May 14 in Dunedin, Florida after Jensen's Hammerhead team finished playing the Dunedin Blue Jays. At the time Jensen was among the leaders in home runs in the Florida State League and was an early season favorite for MVP. Unfortunately he was hit in the hand the day before this interview and the injury took him out of action for a few games.

Let's start with the hand. What happened?

My first at-bat I was deep in the count and the pitcher threw a change-up that went up and in. It hit me right in the palm of my top hand.

What's the diagnosis?

Just a contusion and a bone bruise.

Any idea when you will be back?

It's just day-to-day now.

I have a few questions I wrote before I heard you got hurt. You were selected in the 12th round, does that provide any motivation for you? Especially now with the start you are having?

I just wanted the opportunity to go out and play and show what I can do. It's always good to go out and prove people wrong.

Did you get drafted where you expected? Did you think you were going higher or lower?

I had no idea. There are a lot of things that happen on draft day. You never know what can happen. Things worked out and everything has been good so far.

According to what I read, you started college as a skinny left-handed pitcher and by the end of your college career, you were a power hitting outfielder. How did that happen?

Well, I was going in as a pitcher and I wanted to play both ways and that was in the back of the mind of the coaches at St. Mary's College. Pitching wasn't working out so well by the end of my freshman year, so they said, "Let's stick you in the outfield and see what you can do". Ever since then it's been good.

Last year in Greensboro you were among the leaders in home runs but also in strikeouts. This year you are again among the leaders. Would you say strikeouts and home runs define your game? And you accept the risk for the reward?

Yes and no. You always want to go out there and put the ball in play. That's always a factor. You always to hit the ball hard and that's what it's all about.

Speaking of hitting the ball and putting it in play, you are hitting for a much higher average this year. Is that attributable to a change in approach or are you just putting the bat on the ball more often?

It's staying aggressive and keeping the same plan. Last year I got off to a slow start and this year I have been kind of hot, but you know, baseball has its ups and downs.

You've been hot enough to win organization player of the month, so congratulations on that. What were your reactions when you heard that?

I was surprised at first and it's a good accomplishment, but I just want to continue doing what I've been doing.

Logan Morrison was here in Jupiter for the last week on rehab. You guys play the same position. Did he give you any pointers?

Yeah, he gave me a few tips here and there. He brought a lot of good energy to the club. He was only here for a few games, but he's in the big leagues and I want to be there.

Do you have your sights set on replacing him someday?

I'm just trying to do what I am trying to do and let everything take care of itself.

You'll let the big league club worry about that when the time comes, right?

Yeah.

Stolen bases aren't a huge part of your game, but I noticed you have been very successful when you have run. Is that something you take pride in when the opportunity presents itself?

Yeah, when the manager gives me the go. I try to take the extra base when I see a ball in the gap and other stuff like that.

What do you think you have improved on the most this season and what do you think you need to work on?

Just staying relaxed. I've done a pretty good job so far, but I need to work on that.

How was going from the mound to the outfield? Totally different perspective, right?

It was hard at first, but as you play more games you get more comfortable every day.

So what are your goals for the rest of the season?

Help the team win. To make the playoffs. I'll do whatever I need to do to help them win.

Finally, how do you like Jupiter?

I like it. The area is really nice.

Jensen played 109 games with Jupiter, hitting .309 with 22 homeruns and 66 RBI. His performance earned him the Florida State League's Player of the Year award and a promotion to Double-A Jacksonville (where he hit .250 with five homeruns and 10 RBI in 21 games).

--Mike Lortz

Colin Kaline
Connecticut Tigers (Detroit Tigers)

I spoke with Colin Kaline on August 8 for the New York-Penn League Notebook that appeared at MiLB.com on August 12. The reason I chose Kaline as my focus for that week was because his grandfather, Hall of Famer Al Kaline, was visiting Connecticut that day and I thought it made for an interesting story. Also, my grandfather passed away 17 years ago on August 12.

I was actually quite lucky to speak with Colin, as I arrived in Norwich after the conclusion of his pregame press conference. Tigers Media Relations Manager Justin Sheinis was nice enough to check in frequently on Colin's availability, and the infielder ultimately took several minutes from his game preparation to speak with me.

Your name makes you a bigger story than your average 26th-rounder. Does it get to be a bother with people constantly asking about your family, about your grandfather?

You know, not really. I've made it a point in my mind to know that I am my own player and to respect what he did for this organization, cause it's an unbelievable thing, but also know that I have a long way to go, being a 26th-rounder, and just to keep working hard and doing my thing.

How far did your dad go as a player?

He played through college at Miami of Ohio.

He must get a lot of the same questions that you do, through his life – "Did you play?" "Oh, you're Al Kaline's son." Did he have anything to say as far as handling that sort of stuff?

213

Just to take it how it is. There's going to be critics all the time. There's going to be positive things said and negative things said, so don't get too high or too low when anyone says anything.

Do you ever feel like people expect you to be a player that you're not because of who your grandfather is?

When I was younger I felt that way. As I've grown older and kind of grown into my own player, I think people start to respect and know what to expect of me. Because I do have a completely different style of play. I'm not a big guy, and moving to the infield, so it's completely different.

Are you and your grandfather close?

Yes. I have a very good relationship with him.

Did he ever sit you down at some point and say what you just said: "Listen, you're your own guy, don't listen to what other people say?"

Absolutely, he's been big in making sure that I know that I'm my own player, and not trying to do anything that is out of my repertoire.

This may sound funny, but was there a point when you started realizing that he was more than your grandfather, that he was somebody who meant something to other people?

I can't think of one specific point, but each year I grew older I started to get a better understanding. Especially moving up through the baseball ranks to different levels, you start to have an appreciation for the history of the game, and then you really start realizing what he meant.

There's several baseball families represented here, just in your clubhouse. Is that something that you guys ever talk about, or that ever comes up?

No, not really. All of us are very close as teammates, as young adults. It comes up every once in a while, just a similar story here or there, but it's not really brought up as a central topic.

So it's mostly a guy talking about his brother who happens to play ball or something?

Absolutely.

You were also drafted in 2007 out of high school. Was there any chance of you signing back then?

No, education had always been preached to me, and going in the 25th round out of high school was a great honor, especially being picked by the Tigers, but my family and I pretty much decided right away that I was going to go to school and get a degree.

I read that when you were drafted, your grandfather was the one who called and gave you the news that you were going to be part of the organization. What did that mean to you, that somebody you were so close to, that you had such a close personal relationship with, got to make that call?

It was very special. There's the immediate excitement of being drafted and knowing that you're going to be a professional ballplayer, and then to hear it from somebody that means so much to me made it even more of a special moment.

You're noted for your work ethic and your intellect. What other tools do you bring to the table, both tangible and intangible?

I like to think that I have a good sense, or a good feel, of what's going on with the flow of the game. Being able to read situations and being able to technically execute little things, maybe get a guy over, something like that. Because I have to be able to do that, especially for my size. I don't have the five tools that are preached all the time and that you see some of these young kids possess.

Kaline hit .222 in 39 games for the Connecticut Tigers. He finished with a .328 on-base percentage thanks to 19 walks.

--Originally posted August 18, 2011 by Brian Moynahan

Jeff Locke
Altoona Curve (Pittsburgh Pirates)

One of the big stories at the Eastern League All-Star Game in Manchester, New Hampshire, was the return of local product Jeff Locke, a North Conway native who had never pitched professionally in his home state. Prior to the game, Locke and I spoke for a few minutes about what it meant to come home. His comments were later used in a feature story for MiLB.com.

What does it mean for you to come back here, to your home state, as an All-Star?

It's an honor, any time you get a chance to come back, play in New Hampshire, play in your home state. I've never pitched here before in my life. I played one game and lost, senior year in high school.

That was 2006?

2006, yeah. So I've never had a chance to pitch here. I've had more at-bats here than anything. It's kind of weird, but you know, it's an honor to come back here and be able to play in front of friends and family, especially with a group of talented guys like we have over here. So tonight's just going to be a night of fun, a night of relaxation, watch some homeruns, and have some fun.

You were supposed to pitch here a couple weeks ago, right? And then Mother Nature started acting up? How frustrating was that for you?

I don't think it was as frustrating for me as it was the X amount of people that were coming. I don't live close to here, being from North Conway. I mean, it's not far, but it's a hike, it's a little ways away, and people who were taking work off, who were planning to come, it kind of messed them up a little bit. It didn't bother me a whole lot. I would've liked to go that night, because instead I got on a bus for eight hours and had to pitch the next day and was tired. You know, didn't really frustrate me as much as them. I just wanted to get in and get my innings in and get my work in and go from there. But everything's feeling good. It's frustrating of course but tonight, get my inning to go and I'll be excited.

What's the cheering section looking like tonight? How many people we got coming out?

I left three tickets. I left one for my girlfriend, her dad, and a friend. And my family bought tickets, all of my other family bought tickets. There will be people , for sure – there will be a lot of people for sure – not as if I was starting a game, like a team game, not like that, but it'll be very exciting nonetheless. You could see anything from 20 to 500. It could be anywhere, who knows? I have no idea.

You pitched in Portland last year, right, for a game, and I heard you had a pretty big turnout there.

Just below 2,000 [supporters] showed, and that was a lot of fun. I mean, that's like pitching a home game. And pitching in Portland anyway is kind of like pitching a home game, period, because I grew up going to Sea Dogs games my whole life. Season ticket guy, even when I was a little kid, so it's always an honor. Always a good opportunity to come back to your home state, get a chance to perform, and play a game.

You mentioned that it's not like a game you're starting, but do you know when they're going to use you tonight?

Fourth inning.

Fourth inning. Okay, you're scheduled to go one inning then.

Just the one. Hopefully the one. Hopefully it doesn't go any less than that.

What do you think it's going to be like when you get out there on the mound for the first time, having never pitched in your home state, professionally?

I don't know. I know when I got to Portland, my mouth was all messed up. I couldn't even swallow. That's obviously a lot different than being able to pitch in an All-Star Game, but I don't know. It'll be exciting. Won't be any sense of nervousness. I don't have anything to prove to anybody. I don't need to go out there and throw a scoreless inning or a hitless inning. I don't have to do any of that stuff. I just have to go out there, get the inning over with, have fun. People pay here to see strikeouts and homeruns. That's why they come to All-Star games. It's a chance for the fans to see all the best players in the Eastern League go at it and we'll crown somebody a winner.

How and when did you find out you were going to be on the team?

The day before rosters came out, or I guess the day before they announced them, the manager [P.J. Forbes] had our list of guys. Just post-game meeting, just announced our names. Of course, being the champion of the league last year, it's our staff that will manage, so they told all five of us from Altoona that we would be going to the game. And I think that was the day before they released rosters, or the night before they released them online, so when he found out he told us who was going and to make accommodations and to be professional.

You've been an All-Star before – last year, in the Florida State League? Was there a difference in knowing that you'd be coming home?

Yes. I knew that the All-Star Game was in New Hampshire, last year. Like I knew last year that this year's All-Star Game would be here. And I knew that I only pitched half a year in Double-A last year, and things were starting to look like I'd either start the year in Double-A and do really well and move, or I stay for as long as

I stay and maybe get a chance to play in the All-Star Game. That opportunity has come, and especially after not being able to pitch a couple weeks ago here, just seemed to figure it out the right way. It's an honor, it's going to be a lot of fun. Whether it's the first inning, ninth inning, it's going to be somewhere right in the middle there. It'll be a lot of fun so I'm excited.

Locke became New Hampshire's 51st Major Leaguer (and fourth active with Chris Carpenter, Sam Fuld, and Brian Wilson) when he made his debut against the Marlins on September 10. That high point came on the heels of a season in which he was 7-8 with a 4.03 ERA in 23 games for Double-A Altoona and 1-2 with a 2.22 ERA in five games for Triple-A Indianapolis.

--Brian Moynahan

Richard Lucas
Brooklyn Cyclones (New York Mets)

The fourth round pick of the Mets in the 2007 Draft, Lucas had the distinction of being drafted further back than any other participant in the 2011 New York-Penn League All-Star Game. He spoke with me for a few minutes before the game for a sidebar that appeared on MiLB.com.

So you were the Mets fourth-round pick back in 2007. What was your Draft day experience like?

Draft day, I just had everybody in the house, sitting by the computer, waiting to see it on the Internet, so when it came up it was just crazy. I never knew what it was going to feel like. It definitely was a great experience for me.

Was there ever any doubt you were going to sign a contract, or was there a chance you were going to play college ball?

Money wasn't a real big issue for me. As a little kid, I always talked about playing professional baseball. I had interest in college – I signed with Florida State – but when I was growing up I would never say, "I want to play college baseball." I always talked about playing professionally. So to me money wasn't a big deal. I was just ready to play professional baseball, and I got a good enough opportunity.

It looked like last year the Mets tried to push you up to St. Lucie, and you struggled a little bit. What happened there?

Last year I got up there and started out pretty good the first couple weeks, then I just tried to do too much every time up at the plate. Just trying to do more than I was capable of doing at the time. Just every pitch, trying to hit a homerun, usually got out of my rhythm, got out of my old approach.

So what adjustments did you have to make to get yourself back on track?

I spread out a little bit, just to take my load down a little bit. Just keep my hands not as much in motion. Just calmed everything down a little bit, stayed more patient.

It sounded like you were trying to do too much and trying to be something you weren't at the time. Was it disappointing then this year to come back down to Brooklyn to play there?

I'm not going to say it was disappointing. I mean, I had expectations for myself, but as far as the organization goes, they had their own plan. If I'm on the field, wherever I was going to go I was going to just go out there and give it all I had.

You talk about your plans versus the organization's plans. Coming into this year, do you feel like you had more to prove to you, that you could be a successful ballplayer, or did you have more to prove to them, that you could be successful?

As far as proving anything to myself, I've always had confidence in myself. I know last year was a down year for me, but at the same time I know that I was still better than what I showed last year. I think it was more showing them that I wasn't that guy last year, that it was just a bad year.

And this year has been a good year. You had a five-hit game last month, All-Star appearance now. What does it mean to you to have the opportunity, you're coming out here today, you get to play this game, you've got some recognition as one of the best young guys in this league? What does that mean to you?

It's been a great experience for me. This is my first All-Star Game, so I'm just enjoying everything out here. And the team out in Brooklyn, everybody's playing well, great team out there, good chemistry. It's just been a fun experience this whole year for me.

Yeah, you guys got a good thing going down there. I thought Staten Island was running away with it, but every time I look now, you guys are lurking.

We're starting to put everything back together again. Just playing hard as a team, having fun out on the field, and good things are happening right now.

You're only 22 years old and it's already your fifth season. Do you think that sometimes people kind of forget to take your age into account when they're evaluating you and they say, "Oh this guy, I don't know if he's going to make it."? Do you ever just want to be like, "Dude, I'm 22?"

I hear it a lot. You hear the people saying, "Ah, you're not going to make it." You can't help but look on the Internet sometimes and obviously it's all out there, people saying, "You're not going to make it, you're not going to make it," this and that, but I've been told that a lot before. Even before I got drafted, they told me I wasn't going to get drafted, they told me I wasn't going to get a scholarship. That's just more motivation just to go out there and play hard. I don't really worry about age too much, man. I know I'm 22. I just play as hard as I can every day. That's it.

Lucas hit .300 with six homeruns and 41 RBI in 69 games to help lead Brooklyn to the New York-Penn League playoffs, where they lost to Staten Island in the first round.

--Brian Moynahan

Matthew Neil
Jamestown Jammers (Florida Marlins)

My planned subject for the New York-Penn League Notebook that ran on July 29 was Staten Island's Cito Culver. The Yankees were on the road, however, making it tough to nail down a good time to speak with the shortstop, so I went with Plan B: a 24-year-old rookie named Matthew Neil.

As often happens in situations where one idea fails to pan out, I lucked into a great story, which you will find below. Neil and I enjoyed a lengthy phone conversation in which we talked about his faith, how he started playing college baseball, and his feelings about walks.

You went on a mission a few years ago. I was hoping you could tell me about that.

It was a two-year mission for the Church of Jesus Christ of Latter Day Saints. Some people might know it as the Mormon Church. I went and served in Queens, New York, for a year and then in Long Island for a year, and learned Spanish while I was out there. We would basically just preach the gospel of Jesus Christ to people all over the city, all over the towns, and just invite people to come to church and invite people to come to Christ and explain to them how for me, in my life, growing up there were eight kids in my family. My oldest sister passed away when I was 18. She drowned in a river in California, and it kind of put a little bit of a hardship on our family. And so having the Church in my life, and the gospel, really helps me and gives me strength to realize that this life isn't just about partying every day and doing what you can to be the richest guy around. There's a lot more to it, and it's the people that you get to know. And so just having that, and the experience with my sister, and the example of my parents growing up, I just wanted to go out and share that same message and share the message of the Church with other people as well. And so that's what I did out in New York and for two years I didn't even touch a baseball.

What years was that, when you went?

I was out in New York from April 2006 to April 2008. And then in the fall, in September 2008, I tried out and walked on to the BYU baseball team.

Oh, so you were a walk-on there?

Yeah. So basically from 2005, when my senior year in high school ended, until the summer of 2008, I didn't play baseball at all. Just got back in shape, got my arm back going, and did pretty well the past few years at BYU.

So what were your expectations going into walking-on? I mean, obviously you wanted to make the team, but what were your expectations there?

I knew I could play with those guys. I knew I had the body, I had the arm for it. I feel like I have pretty good accuracy when I throw the ball where I want to, and after not throwing a ball for two years, I came and showed up at the tryouts and hit 90 on the radar gun. And the coaches looked at me and said, "You know, this guy's 6-foot-6 and he just hit 90, I think we'll give him a shot." That's kind of where it started.

My freshman year there I didn't play a whole lot. I just had about three innings. My junior and senior year I was a starter and threw about 80, 85 innings both of those years.

Yeah, I noticed you spent some time as a reliever and as a starter, and you're primarily a starter now. Which role is better for you? Which role do you enjoy more?

I think each of them have their perks. I've been a starter growing up my whole life, all through high school. I enjoyed starting at BYU. But as a reliever I feel like I take a slightly different approach. When I know I'm on the slate to come into the game, I kind of stay relaxed for a while and then whenever my name's

225

called, that's when I get more focused. I feel like I come into the game as a reliever with more intensity, and it's more of just, "throw the ball hard, strike as many people out as I can." But as a starter, I like being able to go through the lineup multiple times because from one at-bat to the next, next time through the lineup, you can set up the hitter. Not only can you set up a hitter between pitches, you can throw him outside and then inside and then inside again, or whatever you want. In a single at-bat, you can set him up from at-bat to at-bat, and I feel like it gets easier for me to either strike people out or get them out after I've faced them in a game.

So for me, I like starting, I'd much rather be a starter than a reliever, but sometimes the competitiveness inside me wants to be a reliever because when the game's on the line and it's a tense situation, I want to be that guy to go in. I did that a few times at BYU, whenever it was a close game or we needed to get out of a tough spot, I was one of the go-to guys there. I like doing that. I like being put in pressure situations and getting out of it. There's just something about it. Gets me fired up.

I find it interesting that you say that as you go through the lineup you find it easier to get guys out because I noticed that three of your starts this year have been against Batavia, and you've started twice against Auburn. Do you feel like that's sort of the same thing, like the more you see the same hitters the more success you have against them?

Yeah, you've just got to be a student of the game. That's why I think it's easier as the game goes on. The pitcher, when you're throwing and you throw a fastball in, you see their swing and you see their body leaning in or out or whatever they're trying to do, you can learn from that and it stays in your mind a lot better. Sometimes when you're just sitting in the bullpen or sitting in the stands keeping charts, sometimes your mind's not as focused on the game. But that's something I've been working on lately, is after you've seen him once, you learn that. You see their swing, you see their approach. If they have a 1-2 count, what are they trying to do? If they have a runner on second, what are they trying to do? You almost have to think as a hitter and then think backwards as to what you want to do to prevent them from trying to be successful.

The more you see hitters, the more you learn their tendencies, and every hitter has a tendency. So as a starter, getting to see them – maybe you started against them in a game five days ago and you get to see them again, that's an advantage, or as a starter once you see their first at-bat you know how to get them the second at-bat or the third at-bat. And if they have success against you in a certain at-bat, you learn from that and make it so they don't get a hit and don't get on base the next time around.

Now one of the other things I noticed about your season so far – you looked like you had good control in college, and you've kind of taken it to another level this year with Jamestown. You've got 33 strikeouts and just two walks. And both those walks were in the same game, so you've gone actually six starts where you haven't walked anybody. Are you at a point right now where it's like you're just putting the ball wherever you want it, or is there another reason for the disparity there?

I feel like I'm putting it where I want it. I feel like whenever I'm locked in and ready to go, I can throw the ball within an inch or two of where I want it. The struggle that I've run into and most of the hits that I've given up this year have been on sliders. I get 0-2 or 1-2 on somebody and I just throw a slider over the middle of the plate. I need to bury my sliders a little bit more.

I'd rather take my chances against them trying to hit it rather than walking them. Walking them, your defense can't play defense. If I get 3-1 or 3-2, I'm going to throw it – it'll be low, I'll work low still – but I'm going to throw it middle part of the plate, maybe outer half of the plate, but I'm not going to try to throw it on the black with three balls. I'm going to force them to earn their place on base.

What pitches do you throw now?

Just four. I throw four-seam fastball, a circle change, a slider and a spike curveball.

What would you say is your best pitch?

I don't know. I mean, fastball I can throw where I want. I feel like I can throw inside and outside on people well. I consider it a strong point. I feel like my curveball is working pretty well. There's a big difference between the college baseballs and the Minor League baseballs that we're using. The seams are a lot smaller here. I feel like my curveball gets a lot more break on it. In college I threw a lot of sliders, a majority of sliders, and now here it's more curveballs. And just working on my changeup still, getting that more developed, but I'd say fastball number one, then curveball.

One of the other things I wanted to ask you was about your Draft experience this year. What was draft day like for you? Did you go higher or lower than you were expecting? Were you expecting to be taken? What was going on that day?

I knew I was a senior for eligibility. I kind of got snookered out of a year with some NCAA mix-up with rules and stuff, so I only got to play three years in college. So I knew as a senior, there'd been 13 or 14 teams that I'd talked to and met with different area scouts for those teams, so come Draft day I knew I wasn't going to be in the top two rounds but I knew I had a chance to do well and as it came on a few of the different teams were calling me on the second day and just saying, "Are you still willing to do this? Do you want to do this even though you're going to be a senior-sign and not going to get a lot of money?" And I said, "I'm just ready to play baseball. I want to play. I feel like I can compete with the best of them."

228

So when my name was called it was pretty exciting. You dream as a kid growing up, of playing professional baseball, and everybody talks about being in the World Series, bottom ninth. And all the things that go through your head as a little kid, it starts somewhere, and the Draft and being picked by the Florida Marlins was a big step in that direction. Pretty exciting.

Your background, with taking a couple years off, generally means you're a little bit older than most of your teammates. Does that affect things in the clubhouse at all? Is there any way that that affects things off the field?

I feel like it helps me more than anything. One, I learned Spanish, and there's a few guys on our team that don't really speak any English, so I feel like I can connect with those guys. And also just being older, I've got a little more life experience. I've lived away from home. I lived on my own basically for two years in New York, and I've done college. So I have the life experience to know people for who they are and not judge them too quickly, and just get to know people. I feel like it's helped me in the clubhouse to be able to get to know my teammates and have fun, to be more of a people person, get to know them and just enjoy the time. I feel like I've meshed and gotten mixed in with these guys rather well.

I can tell you're very passionate about your religious beliefs and everything. Now that you're playing professionally, do you use your status as a ballplayer now to sort of continue the work that you began on your mission? Spreading the word and all that?

I don't look at it as, now I can spread the word, spread the gospel. I look at it as, I'm going to be the person that I am. I have beliefs – I don't drink, I don't smoke, I don't use foul language, I go to church on Sundays when we don't have early games. I try to live my life the way – I try to be more Christ-like. I know I'm not perfect, I know I have a lot of flaws, but I'm out here playing professional baseball and I just want to be me. If somebody sees that and has some questions about why I don't go out with the guys every night or why I don't do some things or why I DO do some things in a different way, then I'll explain to them why I do that, and explain to them my beliefs. But I'm not trying to convert my team. I'm just trying to be the best person that I can and be a good example for those around me.

Neil continued to exhibit fine control, finishing his time in Jamestown with five walks in 66 1/3 innings. He was promoted to High-A Jupiter in late August and made two starts for the Hammerheads, walking two and striking out ten in 10 1/3 innings.

--Originally posted August 3, 2011 by Brian Moynahan

Matt Rice

Hudson Valley Renegades (Tampa Bay Rays)

I first spoke with Matt Rice shortly after the 2010 Draft, when he was the 1,525th and final player selected. He returned to Western Kentucky for his senior year, had a terrific season, and was redrafted in the ninth round by the Tampa Bay Rays.

When I realized Rice was in the New York-Penn League, I knew I had to speak with him for the NYPL Notebook, which ran on July 15. We spoke about the difference between his two Drafts, his approach to his professional career, and the adjustments he has made to life in the minors.

What was this year like compared to last year, in terms of Draft day?

You know, I had a little more of an idea of how it was going to go this year compared to last year. Last year there were obviously a lot of academic issues and signability issues that had to be considered. Once you've been through the Draft one time you kind of get a better feel for how it's going to happen and everything. I was excited this year because I knew I was going to get an opportunity to play and I thought I was going to have an opportunity to go a whole lot higher, obviously, than the last pick. So I was excited coming into the Draft.

It's funny, most guys say that there were signability issues because of academics, they're talking because they're not doing well in school. But you had the opposite problem.

Yeah, I put a lot of work in to that point, and having my major and putting the amount of work it was going to take a significant amount to get me to forgo that senior year. But I think it worked out for the best.

Did you have an idea that Tampa Bay was looking at you?

No, I really didn't. Usually you have meetings with the scouts that are in your area and I hadn't had the opportunity to meet with the guy in my region. They [Tampa Bay] took Kes [Carter] so early, and it's pretty rare that they take two guys from the same team, especially that high, so I really didn't think there was that much of a chance. But it was a pleasant surprise, obviously.

Coming in here to Hudson Valley, what was your mindset as far as what you had to do?

I just wanted to come in here and gain the respect of my teammates and the coaches and just be a guy that goes out there and plays hard and plays the right way. I've got a bunch to learn, I'm trying to learn as much as I can from the coaches here and just work hard every day.

You've been catching and DHing. Are you looking to stay behind the plate?

Yeah, I'm hoping to stay behind the plate. They've been real good about phasing it in, because I didn't play for probably about a month or so. I had a significant break, and they're extremely good about making sure you're ready to go when you're in there and not just throwing you in there. They're very concerned for your health and what's really best for you as a player.

How's it going adjusting to different pitchers and a different pitching staff?

It's a process, you know, but you got to get out there and you got to catch them to get to know them. And we're learning, and everybody's working hard together to try to make that adjustment.

Academically, how did you end up doing this school year?

I ended up with a 4.0.

There was some talk last year, I think, about a Rhodes scholarship, that sort of thing. Is that something that you ever pursued?

I don't think I'm going to end up pursuing that. It was an opportunity that I had that I was fortunate enough to maybe start the application process, but I didn't feel like that was going to be the best option for me. I really wanted to play baseball, so I haven't really pursued that.

Yeah, because you'd have to take time away from this, right? Couple years?

Absolutely.

As far as adjustments to the minor league life, what have been some of your adjustments so far?

I'm living with a host family now, in Hudson Valley, and that's been great. They're extremely good about helping you make the adjustment to the minor leagues. And also Jared [Sandberg, Hudson Valley's manager]. He's really great about talking with us and making sure we're doing okay and everything. But really, I'd say the biggest difference is probably that you're out here every... single ...day. It's not like college, where you play three days and get a few days off. So that's a big adjustment, but I'm working hard to get used to it.

You're not getting the breaks, not balancing classes and baseball.

Absolutely, but you're balancing more bus trips [laughs].

Yeah, I hear that the travel is one of the toughest parts.

It's just an adjustment. First-year guys aren't used to traveling five hours, then getting out and playing. We'd maybe travel that far but we had an off day as a travel day, for college, but it's just an adjustment, and one that we're working hard to make.

Where are you guys headed after this?

We have our first off day tomorrow. First off day of the season, so we're happy about that.

So no travel, no nothing?

No, we're traveling back home, and then we've got the off day, and then we go to Jamestown.

Oh, so that's not too bad. That's pretty close.

I think actually that's what, six hours? Six hours. So we'll get back probably three or four, we'll get a few hours, and then we leave the next morning to go to Jamestown.

I'm trying to think if there's anything else I was thinking of asking. Obviously the last pick in the Draft thing is pretty cool. I think you were the guy who was redrafted the highest, at least in the last few years anyway, which I think is cool.

Absolutely. It's extremely cool. I'm excited about having the opportunity here with the Tampa Bay organization and working to get better.

Rice (who was, coincidentally, born the same day as fellow Bus Leagues interviewee Mike McDade: May 8, 1989) hit .286 with three homeruns and 21 RBI for Hudson Valley. He played 33 of his 54 games behind the plate, surrendering seven passed balls and throwing out 31% of would-be base stealers.

KES CARTER

This interview with Carter was something of an accident. I had just spoken with Rice and was waiting to ask for a few minutes from manager Jared Sandberg after batting practice when one of the players from the Lowell Spinners walked into the visiting dugout and addressed Carter by name.

I remembered from my pre-interview reading that Carter and Rice were teammates at Western Kentucky, so when the conversation ended, the Spinner left, and Carter sat down on the bench, I sidled over to get his thoughts on Rice. From there, the conversation turned toward Carter's season.

Can you give me your thoughts on Matt Rice?

We're best buds, you know, especially in college ball and coming over to professional baseball. I just think it's great that he got a second chance, especially after going last pick overall last year, then getting picked in the ninth round. I think last year he had an opportunity to go higher, but maybe other teams didn't give him an opportunity because they thought he was all about his major and stuff. He's a real smart guy, got a 4.0 and whatnot, in Mechanical Engineering at that. That's probably one of the reasons they didn't take a chance on him. Definitely happy that he got an opportunity to show his tools, because when you look at the guy you're like, "This guy doesn't look like a baseball player," but he puts up ridiculous numbers. Especially in college and then now, coming over to professional baseball he's been putting up great numbers too. I'm really just happy that he's got a second opportunity to play the game he loves and help the team get some wins. He's showing that he can play at the next level and I'm just excited to be a part of his career up to this point and up into the future, hopefully.

Did you guys give him a hard time at all last year? Obviously there are reasons why you go where he did, but did you give him a little good-natured teasing about it?

Last year he got picked, when I heard about it I called him up, I was like, "Congrats man, got drafted." And he was just kind of joking, "Yeah, man, last pick overall, it's a great honor," just kind of jokingly about it. But he didn't really let that faze him this past year, his senior season. He put up just ridiculous numbers again, just like he did in all three other seasons. He's a great player and a great teammate and I think all these guys on this team have started to realize how good of a person he is, on and off the field. He's just a great guy. I'm privileged to be with him at the next level.

How are you doing this year?

Man, I actually got a fractured tibia. I thought it was a stress fracture. It just bothered me, so I went and got it checked out. Come to find out it was fractured. I played in three games. I didn't play the very first game because that's the way they are with new players coming in. They kind of want you to get a feel for it. I played three games, not the first game but the next three games after that, and I was doing alright, but it was just bothering me. I was like, "Man, this doesn't feel right." So I got it checked out, had an MRI, it was a stress fracture. So I've been trying to stay off it. With that kind of injury, you can't really do anything to rehab it. You've just got to rest it. So I'm just trying to take it easy, trying to stay off it. Should be good to go in another couple weeks. Since it's short season ball, we've got another month or so to go – way more than a month – so just taking it day-by-day.

Was that something from school that started bothering you?

Towards the end of the year, in the conference tournament, it started bothering me. I didn't really think much of it. I had our trainer tape me up. You can do a shin splint tape job, and he did that. It really didn't bother me during the game, it was just coming out the next day kind of bothered me. I didn't really think about it because it was so far into the year, so I just waited.

So it felt just like regular fatigue?

236

Yeah, I guess, I don't know. It felt like regular wear-and-tear, I guess just being on it at all times. And just being a baseball player in college, it's a little more different here. You're playing every day. We've got our first off day coming up tomorrow. Every other day we're bang-bang-bang, every day. I guess it's just the wear and tear, you know? So it's not one particular thing where it started hurting, over time it just kind of builds up and if you don't really do anything about it, it just kind of progresses to the next level. So it's a fracture, but like I said, I'm taking it day-by-day. I don't want to come back too early and have it be bothering me for the rest of the year. I don't want to come back and have another setback.

I'm sure they're thinking the same thing.

That's what's different about pro ball than college ball. I guess there's not as many players at their disposal. They kind of try to rush you back, in college, more so than pro – they want to make sure you're good to go. They care about you, you're there, you're in their business. The organization's looking out for me, they've got my back. Just taking it day-by-day, so hopefully it won't be too much longer than 2 ½ weeks.

It's kind of frustrating, going on the road and suiting up and everything and then just hanging out, but that's what I've got to do.

I work up in Manchester too, with the Double-A team up there, and just talking to some of the guys up there, they hate being injured. You're just doing nothing.

It's frustrating, but you got to stay positive. You've got to keep a positive state of mind, and I'm doing the things I can. In the weight room I'll be doing upper body, low impact stuff like riding the bikes. I ride the bike a lot. Trying to stay in shape as best I can, but like I said I'm not trying to push it. It's feeling better day-by-day and that's the way I'm looking at it, taking it day-by-day. Keep a positive state of mind.

Back to Rice, man, just happy he's got that second opportunity to show what he's got. His swing, it's unorthodox, he's got kind of an uppercut swing, so to speak, and a lot of people didn't really think that would translate to pro ball. He's already got two homeruns, he's second in homeruns behind Jeff Malm, who's actually leading the whole league with six. He's showing what he's got, I couldn't be happier for him.

It's good to hear stuff like that. I like to see a guy doing well. Cause you see guys drafted in that spot and the next year, four years later, they're gone.

He's definitely hit it off with a bang, man. He's really, I wouldn't say hard on himself, but he breaks it down. He's a really intelligent guy and that comes into baseball too. Baseball's so mental. He stays on himself and I have no doubts that his career will go for a long time. I plan on it going for a long time. Hopefully we can move on up the planks together.

It's got to be nice, being college teammates and then coming here.

Yeah, that was kind of cool when I heard about it. I called him up, I couldn't believe it. Obviously drafted, then to be drafted by the Rays, same organization, just amazing. There's actually another guy here, Raymond Church, kid out there at second, he played in our conference, so we knew of each other. He played at Florida Atlantic University, so we knew of each other. That was just another person we could go to, talk to, feel comfortable around.

A guy you've seen around at least.

Yeah. And then there's actually another kid — me and Rice are both from Tennessee, and there's another guy on here, a pitcher,

Andy Bass, he's from Tennessee as well. He's from my area. First day coming out here, we actually knew or had something in common with several different guys. Since then it's a great team, we've got pretty good camaraderie, we're just getting closer and closer each day, and I think that really helps in the long run, especially winning games, being on the same page each and every day.

Yeah, seems like the manager's really laid back.

I guess that's pretty much the way most professional organizations are. I just know, from personal experience, here. He's laid back. He'll get on your ass if he needs to, but he's a good guy. All the coaches and managers are great guys. They've got the experience and they all know what they're talking about, so it's a really great thing to be a part of this organization.

Carter did not return to the field in 2011.

--Brian Moynahan

Garrett Wittels
Batavia Muckdogs (St. Louis Cardinals)

As a sophomore at Florida International University, Garrett Wittels hit safely in 56 consecutive games, the second longest streak in Division I history. The following winter, however, he was involved in legal trouble after being accused of raping a teenage girl while on vacation in the Bahamas. Though the charges were eventually dropped, Wittels went undrafted in 2011, instead signing with the Cardinals as a free agent.

The New York-Penn League Notebook on Wittels appeared at MiLB.com on August 22.

I follow you on Twitter, so I noticed you were in Boston yesterday. You saw the second Sox game?

Yeah I did.

First time at Fenway?

It was actually my second time at Fenway. I went as a kid and really didn't get to appreciate it much because I was young and didn't know too much about baseball. But going back there, it was a great vibe. Being brought up in Miami, sometimes the sports fans aren't too passionate middle of the year. Yeah, they won the World Series a couple times, but it was just kind of crazy to see everyone wearing Red Sox stuff and everyone going to the game and it was just a great experience.

I wanted to talk about the Draft a little bit. What were your expectations going into the Draft this year?

Coming off a pretty good year last year, I expected to get drafted. I didn't really know exactly where, but I heard a lot of things, anywhere from four to 15. Kind of not go too early but kind of in a good spot to get some good money and things like that. Unfortunately it didn't really work out.

240

As you're sitting there going through the day – I'm guessing you were paying attention to what was going on – what's going through your head as they're going through the rounds?

Growing up, I've always played the game passionately, and the one thing I've always wanted to do is be a professional baseball player. You grow up as a kid and you work all the extra hours, you put in all the time in the batting cages, you go out there, the sweat, the blood, all of it, to win, and hopefully one day to be a professional athlete. I had some high expectations for the Draft, especially because I heard it from different scouts. I heard it from my advisor at the time. I heard it from my head coach, Turtle Thomas, who's been around for many years, at my exit meeting a few days before the Draft. He told me that he's heard a lot of good things and he hopes it all works out, things like that.

But when the day came, it was very emotional. 5, 6, 7, 10, 15, 20…second day come and go, and I didn't really know what to think. My advisor told me, "Maybe the best thing for you at this point is not to get drafted so you can pick an organization to go to," and that's basically what happened.

Did you have multiple organizations that were interested after the Draft?

Not after the Draft, but after everything off the field got cleared up a lot of teams started to call. But Charlie Gonzalez, a scout for the Cardinals who's followed me all throughout, he called me and kind of sold me on the Cardinals. They love my kind of player – maybe not the most talented guy, but guys who just go out there and bust their butt every single day and show everything out on the field and just play hard.

You had some pretty well-documented legal issues. Do you feel that played a role in you dropping out of the Draft?

I know it did. I'm not really supposed to talk much about it, but I know it did. Many teams said they couldn't take the publicity, and I just had to deal with it from there.

Correct me if I'm wrong – did you have a year of eligibility left for school?

Yeah I did.

Did you determine before the Draft that you were going to be leaving school or was that a decision you came to after?

I thought it was going to depend on what happened with the Draft. I didn't really expect to go back to school. After I didn't get drafted, then I really just had to say what was the best thing for Garrett Wittels. Once everything got cleared up, I decided that the best thing for me was to go turn pro and get my shot. You never know if you go back to school what can or cannot happen, and I knew that seeing all the guys that got drafted and a lot of my buddies playing I could fit in pretty well. I took my chance and here I am.

Was there ever any concern that there wasn't going to be something there or did you figure everything would work out?

Once I went down to the Bahamas nine days after the Draft and everything got cleared up, a couple days, I went to play ball in Moorhead City in the Coastal Plains League, just to get at-bats and stay fresh, and a couple teams started to call, and that's when I picked the Cardinals.

So you felt there was going to be an opportunity there, it was just a matter of keeping yourself in shape.

I had an idea about signing as a free agent. A lot of teams told me that once the off-the-field things finished up and was gone that it would be a different story about playing professional baseball, and once that cleared up I knew that I was just going to try to get myself in shape, get some good at-bats, and hopefully get ready to sign as a free agent. But if not, just go back to school and help my team try to win a championship.

I read that religion is important to you. That's something that caught my eye because I was a Religious Studies major in college. Can you talk about the role that it plays in your life?

It's not that I'm really religious. I'm just kind of spiritual. I believe in God, I believe in the Baseball Gods. I'm just a very spiritual person. I believe in karma, things like that, the way you carry yourself. Kind of make your own luck, really.

I am Jewish. I know they're making an Israeli World Baseball Classic team, someone mentioned it to me, and hopefully I can somehow get on that roster with some of the guys like Ian Kinsler, Jason Marquis, Kevin Youkilis, Ryan Braun, things like that. It'd be very special for me and it'd be a great opportunity.

I mentioned the hitting streak when we first started talking. Can you describe what it's like to experience a long hitting streak from the perspective of the guy who's having the streak?

Honestly, at the time I was just kind of zoned in. Now, looking back, I just saw Dan Uggla with a 33-game hit streak and I see guys like that, I realize how hard something like that really was. But at the time I was just zoned in on winning games and playing well that at the time I just really didn't think about it too much. I tried to just go out there every day. It's never easy to get hits, but there are times during the season when you're seeing the ball well. The ball just kind of finds the barrel, I guess.

I'm guessing it became more difficult as more attention came on. You've got ESPN watching you...

I feel like it helped our team a lot. We ended up winning the Sun Belt conference championship at FIU. It was kind of just giving our team energy. The hardest part for me was the seven months after the season. I tried not to think about it much, but every single person I ever talked to on an everyday basis would always bring it up, and it was kind of just something there in your head.

But like I said, at the time the whole streak was going on during the 2010 season, I really didn't think of it that much. Yeah, I thought about it maybe if I was 0-for-3, 0-for-4, but early on in the game I was just trying to play good baseball and hit the ball hard.

There's not a lot of guys who can tell you what it feels like to go that long with a hitting streak.

It's easy to have a plan, really. Every day I got to the stadium around the same time, hit off the tee a little bit, hit a little bit of front toss, just really tried to stay fresh, not take too many swings to get myself out of being so hot, and not take too few swings. As a hitter, you kind of know when you're ready to go. There were days that my head coach would be like, "Come on Garrett, you've got to take a couple more swings in BP," or, "That's good," things like that. He kind of knew when I was ready to go or not.

I know it hasn't been very long since you've been out of school, but is there any way you've changed as a player since college? Changed your approach or your routine, anything like that?

Playing professional baseball is a lot different than college ball. In professional baseball it's all on you, really. If you want to hit extra, if you want to hit before, it's all on you. The coaches aren't going to tell you to go hit, like it is in college. But like I said, I look at myself as a grinder, so I always get my work in when I need to get my work in and when I'm feeling good, try not to take too many swings. Just go out and play hard, really.

It's a little bit more of an individual game in pro ball. A lot of guys are more selfish because they're trying to do what they can do to move up in the organization. But just try to play hard every single day and win every day and that's what I focus on.

Wittels spent 42 games with Batavia, hitting .262 and playing four different defensive positions (second base, third base, shortstop, and left field).

--Brian Moynahan

From the Podcast

Jackie Bradley, Jr.

Lowell Spinners (Boston Red Sox)

The 40ᵗʰ overall pick in the 2011 Draft out of the University of South Carolina, Bradley signed at the August 15 deadline and reported to Lowell days later. He was the first player featured on the Bus Leagues Podcast.

Looking through the stats, I saw only one college program going back to the 1930s has ever won three straight College World Series. You guys at South Carolina, you won two in a row. Was it hard to actually sign a professional contract and say you're not going to go back to school and go after that third straight title?

Um…you know, I don't think either option was hard for me. I'm a pretty level guy, I'm never really too amped up to do one particular thing. But I would've been perfectly fine with going back to college. I was at a great program, great coaches, great teammates, and I'd love to make that third run. But the way everything has happened the past few weeks, I just got the opportunity that I couldn't really pass up, and everybody understands that. I've had a great successful three years in college, and I'm proud to where I've come a long way from high school, and college as well.

I know there's a lot of stuff that goes into it when you're making that decision to sign, there's a lot of different factors that you're pulling together. I noticed that you had some injuries. Every year it seemed like you had something pop up. How much of a factor was the injury risk in going back for your senior year?

It wasn't really paying a toll on me. I know a lot of people probably talk about injuries, but if you're even thinking about it, only one of my injuries was baseball-related, and that was this past injury that I had with my wrist. I did that diving at Mississippi State. My freshman injury, I had an extra rib. You know, it has nothing to do with baseball. I just had to get an extra rib removed. My sophomore year, a hamate bone removal, and that's pretty common in baseball and golf players. So that's really nothing too big. But this past one, I did have a slight tear in my ligament, which caused my tendon to come out of the sheath compartment. Everything's all fixed, I'm back on the field. I was back a lot of weeks ahead of time, not because I rushed it back on or anything like that, it's just because I felt good. I did everything I was supposed to do and it just happened that, it was just basically like a miracle. I was able to come back from all three of my injuries ahead of time, and it's just a blessing how it all came together.

Yeah, when you said that I started to think that I read about your hand, it said that you came back very quick, so it seems like you heal quickly at least.

Yeah, I guess that's my superpower, healing.

Between the College World Series and the signing deadline, you had a little bit of a gap in there where there was really free time, I guess. What did you do to fill the gap in that month and a half or so?

Mostly just hang out with family, enjoy the family, since this was the first summer that I actually didn't have to play ball. Every other summer before then I was constantly on the go. But I was also staying in shape. I think some of the people might think that I was taking off or something. Of course I was taking off time to let my actual wrist heal completely up, get it stronger and get it strengthened back up to where I needed to be. But I was constantly working, taking BP with my old team back in high school, coaches. I was doing a workout called Insanity as well, so I was definitely not being a couch potato, I was definitely getting after it, because I wanted to be ready for whatever was next.

And next turned out to be signing and coming down to Lowell – or coming up to Lowell, as it were. What's your

routine been like since you got here? You've been here about a week or so, right?

Yeah, I think today's my sixth day. I've pretty much hopped into it pretty fast. I think I was on the plane two days after...well actually, a day after the deadline, but then I guess the deadline's at midnight. It all just happened so fast. Put into a new system and just getting acclimated to everything. But it's something I'm definitely getting used to, and I love being on the field every single day. I think that's how it should be. You treat your body right and this game will reward you. It's all about longevity. In order to be prepared for every single day you've got to train for it.

Do you think the transition for you, coming from a major Division I college program, do you think that's easier than a kid who might be coming to Lowell out of high school or a lower division program?

It might be. With a bigger school, you're used to the crowd and all the hoopla and all the stuff like that. I think at our school, we got something close to 8,000 fans. So it's pretty big, and just everybody supporting you. Baseball has really come a long...well, we've always been really good at South Carolina baseball, but these past couple years have just been an unbelievable run, which our fans really appreciated. We were able to bring our university the first and second national championships out of the three main sports. And they're real appreciative. When you have older people telling you they've waited 50 and 60 years, and they didn't ever think that it was going to be able to come in their lifetime, how much it meant, and they're crying, grown men are crying. It really meant something special. So coming here, I'm glad that I was able to be a part of that particular program and what it was all about.

I was going to ask you if there's any added pressure being a Red Sox draft pick because baseball's so huge in "Red Sox Nation" and all that, but it sounds like you're coming from a similar situation.

Yeah, I've heard a lot of talk about the Red Sox fans being tough and stuff like that, but why would you want it any other way? You don't. You don't want the fans to be soft on you. You're here to perform at a high level, and there's a lot of expectations put on you by being a Red Sox, and I'm perfectly fine with that. You're human, everything's not perfect, they understand that as well. They want to know, and put their faith in you, that you're a pretty good ballplayer, so you got a job to do.

So you're scheduled on Wednesday, to make your debut?

I believe so, Wednesday's the day.

Any nerves yet? Or are you just chomping at the bit to get out there?

No, no nerves for me. I'm ready. I've been playing baseball for I don't know how long, so I don't really get too nervous anymore. I just get excited, and ready for the next opportunity. I want to take advantage of every single opportunity that I get. Every single at-bat, every single pitch. Just putting things into perspective. A lot of people don't get to do what we do, and a lot of people dream to be where we are, and I'm at the point where by me being able to do this, there's a lot of other people looking at me and just saying, "You're living through me vicariously." And I'm ready to go on about it.

Just to close it out: for the rest of this season, for next year, on into next year, what are your goals? What are some of the things you hope to accomplish here?

Just be myself. That's the main thing, to be myself and be healthy. Everything else will fall into place.

Bradley started his career a day earlier than expected, debuting with Lowell the day after we spoke. He hit .190 (4-for-21) in six games for the Spinners before being promoted to Low-A Greenville, where he hit .333 (5-for-15) in four games.

--Brian Moynahan

Jeff Perro
Birmingham Barons Clubhouse Manager

After last year's extensive email interview, we had Jeff back this season as the first guest on our podcast.

I appreciate you taking the time out.

No problem. It's a Saturday off during the baseball season. I've been pretty much doing nothing all day. I don't mind.

A Saturday off during the baseball season? How often do you get that luxury?

Um, I guess about once or twice a month, maybe. Yeah, about once or twice a month.

That's not too bad. What's the season been going like so far?

From my point of view, the season's been going well. I seem to have a better group of guys every season that I've been here. This is my third year here, and I have a good group of guys and we just happen to have a lot of fun. From the team point of view, we won the first half in the Southern League South Division, and it's just fun because we kind of started off the season a little slow, won a bunch of games to come out on top of the standings, so that was great. The second half, we struggled on the field a little bit, but I still think our team has the personality and the attitude to win. We didn't really have a lot of personnel changes down here, so there's that. I think we've got to start winning some games on the field and get some positive energy, positive thoughts going towards the playoffs.

How does the clubhouse atmosphere change between when your successful like you were in the first half versus when you're struggling a little bit more in the second half?

The atmosphere isn't that much different. Like I said we haven't had a whole lot of changes in personnel, and our guys are always staying positive. We've had some tough losses, errors, crappy umpiring, some stuff like that, the usual things that happen. Just all the breaks haven't gone our way, but we still win the occasional game

In 2009 we won the division also, and we had one of the top three, top five records in all of Minor League Baseball. Last year we had a completely different team and were probably in the bottom five out of all the records in Minor League Baseball. That's a really weird atmosphere change from year to year. When the team's winning, losing sucks. You can hear a pin drop, after you lose a tough game when your team's been winning. Once you get a few losses in you like we did last year losing still hurts, but well we have another one tomorrow. After you get enough losses and you kind of head down that road, you'll get them tomorrow, maybe you do and eventually you don't.

What do you do to affect the attitude; does your attitude impact the other guys?

I'd like to think I do. One of the things - I didn't put this on my resume - four of the five years I've been clubhouse manager, the team's made the playoffs. I would like to think there's some sort of correlation there, or maybe my attitude or mentality helped with that. You kind of have to read the team a little bit. Sometimes we have a really "rah rah" dugout and sometimes we don't. If I can tell I can go hang out in the dugout for a few innings during the game and give a little positive vibe and "rah rah" going. Other times I'm kind of the clubhouse enforcer type. We have the organizational policies, the TV goes off at 6:30 for seven o'clock games, and some teams need the focus, some teams need the putting away the ping pong, turning off the TV at 6:30. Every team has to have fun. We can have fun at five o'clock during BP (batting practice), and goof around and be jackasses. That might be what the team needs. But that involves reading the team's personality; I have enough personality and wit to be able to read the situation.

That's got to be an important characteristic to be good at what you do, be able to roll with the punches, pick people up, at the same time be a leader both on and off the field.

I agree. That's why it's more than just a job to me. It's something that I'm passionate about, that I enjoy doing. I enjoy being apart of a team atmosphere, I enjoy winning.

You're coming into a free agency period at the end of the season, what is the process like? Do you look for jobs or leads during the season or wait until the end of the year? What goes through your head because obviously the offseason isn't too long between the end of this year and the start of next season? What are you doing now and what are you doing to prepare for next season?

I really don't plan on doing much until after the season, we have a good network of clubhouse managers in Minor League Baseball, just working together changing leagues, we have a good network of about 50 guys and a close network of about 12 to 15 guys. I've already heard that so-and-so will be open next year, so-and-so was fired for doing this. I'm hearing things. It's all in who you know. I've already started to get my leads going on, I have my guys that I've started networking with and talking to general managers about job openings. I'm starting to figure out what jobs will be better and what jobs won't be better.

Is that a big goal for you to move up amongst the minor leagues and eventually getting to the major leagues? Is it like moving up through a farm system?

My goal is a little bit different. I grew up around major league baseball, we had (Texas) Rangers season tickets, toward high school I started hanging out around Minor League Baseball and that became my passion. I enjoy Minor League Baseball more. I like the atmosphere of Minor League Baseball more than the major league atmosphere. My ultimate goal is to make it to the major leagues and work for the Boston Red Sox in Fenway. My goal is to work for a spring training facility, maybe in Arizona or Florida in the Florida State League, between rookie ball or instruction league or camp to spend the year working in Minor League Baseball.

The majority of the guys have goals to make it to the big league, that's really tough as a clubhouse manager. For instance Mike Murphy in San Francisco, he's been there I want to say 40-50 years, and he kind of became a celebrity during the World Series for being there for so long. Clubhouse managers don't retire, they die. The turnover for a clubhouse manager at a major league level is much less than a manager or general manager. I don't want to say it's impossible to get there…but it's pretty hard.

The tornadoes this year played a big impact in the Birmingham area. What was the hardest part for you both professionally and personally?

Personally the hardest part was I was here at the ballpark south of Birmingham the night that the tornado hit; we had a neighboring RV park outside of right field and we had the people from the RV park and a few others at the ballpark seeking shelter. My son and his mom live in Fultonville, Alabama, which is about 15 minutes north of town, and of course that's where the path of the tornado went through, the north part of town. So I'm watching it on TV at five or six o'clock at night and I'm trying to call and make sure that things are okay. Finally I get a text message from my son's mom at ten o'clock at night. Those four or five hours watching on TV were pretty stressful. But they made it through okay and everything was alright. I was almost a trainwreck but not quite, I almost panicked but not quite.

That's the hardest part when it specifically affects your family, there's only so much you can do it leaves you with a

bit of feeling of helplessness that you can't do anything until it's all over.

Yeah

What have you seen as far as support from the fans as well as the franchise? I know that New Orleans is a bigger scale picture, but after that the fans and team really came together as one. Have you seen that kind of connection between your team and your fans?

That was the great thing, we had a couple guys from Alabama on the team, but we also had players from California and Miami, where these guys were able to relate even though they were from here. They were more than willing to help out when they could. We spent one day at the relief center passing out pies and helping the efforts. That was a fascinating couple of days doing that, people in the community willing to donate. We were offloading trucks in the summer heat before a game, and people were driving through saying they lost everything, and the Red Cross was passing out cases of food and bottled water and clothes and all that, it was a pretty amazing day doing that.

There is no doubt how big community interaction is in Minor League Baseball.

These guys at the park aren't just local guys, they are from all over the country and once we got there they saw the need for it. They weren't afraid to get dirty together and help out when they could. They had lost everything and needed everything.

How much does something like that, working side-by-side, bring a team together especially before the season?

I think it definitely does. These are the days of the iPods and the headphones and their laptops. This isn't the same clubhouse as it was during the 50's and 60's, where the team was a team and did everything together. It's a different atmosphere now where basically they are a team on the field but off the field they are basically 25 or 30 individuals. So getting into an atmosphere where they work together off the field, it gave them stories and feelings, allowed them to hang out where they otherwise may not hang out together outside the ballpark, that's the cool thing about it. It was a great team bonding experience as well.

I want to end on a light note, where will you be in 2012?

[chuckles] I don't know. I want to move on to something bigger and better. At the same time I do have my five-year-old son living in Birmingham, so there's a chance that I could move away somewhere in California for a great job or I could stay here and buy season tickets to the Barons games. There's a slim chance of that, but hopefully I will get my dream job in Arizona or Florida and talk to my son's mom about coming down and visiting all the time, that would be the ideal situation. I'll go with that. I'll be in Arizona.

We're breaking news right here?

[chuckles] If this was Major League Baseball there would be some tampering going on right now.

I don't want an investigation from the league; I don't want the commissioner looking for me for tampering [laughing]. Thank you for your time and enjoy the rest of the season.

Thanks a lot, give me a call anytime.

Jeff wasn't able to land a clubhouse manager job in Arizona this offseason, but is still in the process of applying for different positions in Minor League Baseball.

--*Chris Fee*

George Springer
Tri-City ValleyCats (Houston Astros)

Springer, the 11ᵗʰ overall pick by the Houston Astros in the 2011 Draft, sat down with me before a game against the Lowell Spinners for an interview that appeared on the second edition of the Bus Leagues Podcast.

Matt Barnes is your old teammate I guess from way back, not even just college. He's with Lowell. I'm assuming you've maybe had a chance to catch up with him a little bit in the last couple days you've been here. What's it like when you see a guy who, he's a great friend and you've shared a lot with him as a teammate, now you're looking at him across the field from the other dugout? What's that like?

Actually, it's a pretty weird feeling. Me and Matt have hung out the last few days, and for the first time in the last six or seven years, he's over there and I'm over here, and that's just something…it's odd to not see him in the same jersey as I have been in the last few years, but I'm happy for him. I'm happy for his situation and I wish him the best of luck here, and hopefully I get to play with him soon enough or play against him.

Do you think it's going to be even a little more weird one day if you actually have to step in against him?

Yeah. I've faced him plenty of times before at school, but I figure the first time when we're in a different jersey and there's a lot more actually at stake, yeah, it'll be weird. Me and him are good friends. He'll probably smile at me and I might say a little something, but it's all fun.

It's like you're going to know what he's going to throw and you're just going to be like, "Yeah, I'm going to hit you."

Yeah, I mean, he's obviously a phenomenal pitcher, but I know him. I've had the privilege to watch him pitch for the last four or

259

five years. He has an incredible arm, he's just an unbelievable kid, so I have an idea of what he'll throw, but hopefully he gets a little bit smarter and switches it up on me.

Leading up to the signing deadline, you met with the Long Island Ducks, in late July. Just like a contingency plan, it sounded like, in case you didn't sign. Other guys have done that in the past – like J.D. Drew, who was here last night, he did it a bunch of years ago – do you think you would've taken that step if you hadn't signed with the Astros?

It's hard to say yes and it's hard to say no. I don't really know what would've happened, but I was very interested in starting my professional career and if that was either with the Astros or somebody else, I honestly can't give you a straight up "no" or "yes". I guess if you want to say, that was an option.

You just wanted to get on the field and play somewhere.

Yeah, yeah.

Again, you signed right at the deadline, but then I was also reading that 10 days before you visited Houston to get your physical out of the way, saw the ballpark. Did that sort of impact your decision to ultimately sign? Did it kind of just stick in your head that, "This is what it's like, I don't want to turn down the opportunity to have this right now"?

It wasn't that it heightened my feeling to sign or anything. That was just an incredible experience as a kid. I mean, I got to do down and see the clubhouse and everything like that. It wasn't, I guess if you want to say, a recruiting trip for me or anything like that. I was hoping to get something done, and it happened on the 15th, and here I am now.

The recruiting part of it was something else. I noticed in the article I read that their GM said, "No, absolutely not, it wasn't a recruiting trip," but you look at everything

together, it's almost like a little good-natured cat-and-mouse between you guys, like, "Oh, we're going to go talk to an independent league team." "Well, come look at the ballpark." Not that there was any malice to it or anything, just a little back and forth.

The physical part is something is mandatory, and I had to get that done just to show that I'm healthy, I'm cleared to go. We got that out of the way and I also had a shot to see the ballpark at the same time.

Back in 2008 you were taken in the 48th round. Obviously you were a lot younger then, but did being drafted in the later rounds of the Draft motivate you to work harder, and not turn you into a first round pick, but motivate you to push yourself more to go higher in a later year?

I don't necessarily say I pushed myself to get myself drafted. It was just one of those things where I was fortunate enough to get drafted as a kid, I guess, and then I just worked hard and things happened and I was really fortunate to have this happen again, just 47 rounds before. I guess yeah, it's an incentive to be the best player that you can be, but being a first round pick isn't something that you dream of, and I was provided with that opportunity. And I'm extremely fortunate for this whole organization giving me the chance to go out and play as a first-round pick and as a Houston Astro.

Yeah, seemed like they were pretty excited to get you, too. From what I was reading they were pretty pumped that you were there when it was your turn to pick.

That's something special to me. Once again, I'm extremely happy to be here, I'm extremely happy to be an Astro, and I'm just going to go out and work as hard as I can.

From what I was reading up on, it seems there's not a lot you can't do on a baseball field, is kind of the best I feel how

to describe it. **What would you say your greatest strength and your greatest weakness are on the field?**

Ah…my greatest strength is that I just go out and have fun. I'm always relaxed. I'm not really too concerned about what happens. This game is already hard enough as it is, and you can't try to be somebody that you're not. And I just go out and I play my game and let the physical stuff happen. My greatest weakness, I would say, is that I sometimes get out in front of myself and don't let the game slow down, don't let the game come to me. The physical part of the game is something that you can't control, so you just got to go out there and react. That's just something that happens. The mental side, letting stuff slow down, learning about this situation and that situation has been something I've been trying to do for the last three to four to five years.

That's interesting that you mention just going out and reacting, because I was watching last night the play you made against South Carolina in the Super Regional. It was a fly ball, hit to center, over your head, and you just went back and made a fantastic catch on it. Are you thinking anything as the ball comes off the bat there and you start to pursue it or is that just all reaction?

My first reaction and thought is, "Go get it." You know what I mean? Go do whatever it is that you have to do to catch the ball, and that's how I am with each fly ball that gets hit. You really can't think that much. It's just, go out and just go track it down somehow.

I read that you were a history major at Connecticut. I was a history major myself, so it interested me. What drew you to that field and did you have any specific focus or concentration in any area?

Just something I was interested in. Just something I was interested in, they had it at school, I went with it.

I think that's what you hear from most history majors.

[laughs] Yeah, right, exactly.

Eh, it was something to do.

Yeah, I had some interest in it, they had it, and I went for it.

Did you finish up your degree or do you still have another year?

I have some semesters left.

Do you plan on going back and finishing at some point?

Yes I do. I plan on it.

I had also read that you were diagnosed when you were younger with a stutter. How old were you when that started and what have you done to overcome it?

I was a kid. I don't really know when that happened, or when I was technically diagnosed, but I don't know, I just slow things down, don't try to speed anything up and I'm good to go.

Just kind of take your time?

Yeah, yup. It's not rocket science. You just speak slowly and if it happens, it happens. I'm not really too concerned about it.

You made your professional debut last night. After a couple months, how did it finally feel to get out there on the field and play a game? What were you feeling before the game?

I was excited. I was excited to get back out there and get my feet wet a little bit. I had three at-bats and played a few innings out in the field, and now I'm ready to go.

263

What's the plan? Where do you go after the season ends?

I will go down to the Instructional League.

That's the one down in Florida?

Yup. And then on from there.

Onward and upward, right?

Yes sir.

Springer played eight games for the Tri-City ValleyCats, hitting .179 (5-for-28) with four stolen bases. He handled 13 chances flawlessly in centerfield.

--Brian Moynahan

Acknowledgements

The majority of the interviews that comprise *The Bus Leagues Experience: Volume 2* were only made possible through the support of Media Relations Managers at all levels of Minor League Baseball.

We wish to extend special thanks to the teams that provided us with full-season media credentials in 2011, including the Tampa Yankees (Matthew Gees), Rochester Red Wings (Chuck Hinkel), Lowell Spinners (Jon Boswell), and New Hampshire Fisher Cats (Matt Leite).

We also must thank the teams that welcomed us into their ballparks, on assignment for both Bus Leagues and MiLB.com, on a game-by-game basis this season, including the Dunedin Blue Jays (Craig Durham), Trenton Thunder (Bill Cook), Connecticut Tigers (Justin Sheinis), Bradenton Marauders (Joel Goddett), Tucson Padres (Tim Hagerty), Auburn Doubledays (John Miller), Syracuse Chiefs (Jason Benetti), and Buffalo Bisons (Brad Bisbing).

Finally, we received assistance from many teams and individuals in setting up phone interviews and conversations away from the ballpark. Those who helped in this regard include Steve Densa (Minor League Baseball), Justin Rosenberg (Norfolk Tides), Joe Putnam (State College Spikes), John McCutchan (Staten Island Yankees), Kyle Smith (Brevard County Manatees), Grant McAuley (Charlotte Stone Crabs), Mike Bauer (Jupiter Hammerheads), and Dan Scotchmer (Jamestown Jammers).

MiLB.com Reference

Lortz, Michael. "FSL notes: Colome coming along." 4 May 2011. http://web.minorleaguebaseball.com/news/article.jsp?ymd=201 10503&content_id=18566362&vkey=news_l123&fext=.jsp&sid =l123.

Lortz, Michael. "FSL notes: Jensen making believers." 18 May 2011. http://web.minorleaguebaseball.com/news/article.jsp?ymd=201 10517&content_id=19180124&vkey=news_l123&fext=.jsp&sid =l123.

Lortz, Michael. "FSL notes: Cunningham powers back." 25 May 2011. http://web.minorleaguebaseball.com/news/article.jsp?ymd=201 10524&content_id=19488348&vkey=news_l123&fext=.jsp&sid =l123.

Moynahan, Brian. "NYPL notes: Allie eyeing control." 1 July 2011. http://web.minorleaguebaseball.com/news/article.jsp?ymd=201 10630&content_id=21209754&vkey=news_l127&fext=.jsp&sid =l127.

Moynahan, Brian. "NYPL notes: Altherr finding his groove." 8 July 2011. http://web.minorleaguebaseball.com/news/article.jsp?ymd=201 10708&content_id=21586296&vkey=news_l127&fext=.jsp&sid =l127.

Moynahan, Brian. "Locke finally gets to pitch at 'home'." 13 July 2011. http://web.minorleaguebaseball.com/news/article.jsp?ymd=201 10713&content_id=21777440&vkey=news_l113&fext=.jsp&sid =l113.

Moynahan, Brian. "NYPL notes: Rice earning respect." 15 July 2011.
http://web.minorleaguebaseball.com/news/article.jsp?ymd=201
10714&content_id=21782286&vkey=news_l127&fext=.jsp&sid
=l127.

Moynahan, Brian. "NYPL notes: Cecchini heating up." 22 July 2011.
http://web.minorleaguebaseball.com/news/article.jsp?ymd=201
10721&content_id=22103726&vkey=news_l127&fext=.jsp&sid
=l127.

Moynahan, Brian. "NYPL notes: Neil on a pitching mission." 29 July 2011.
http://web.minorleaguebaseball.com/news/article.jsp?ymd=201
10728&content_id=22418210&vkey=news_l127&fext=.jsp&sid
=l127.

Moynahan, Brian. "NYPL notes: Hobgood feeling well again." 5 August 2011.
http://web.minorleaguebaseball.com/news/article.jsp?ymd=201
10804&content_id=22738152&vkey=news_l127&fext=.jsp&sid
=l127.

Moynahan, Brian. "NYPL notes: Kaline carries on tradition." 12 August 2011.
http://web.minorleaguebaseball.com/news/article.jsp?ymd=201
10811&content_id=23072712&vkey=news_l127&fext=.jsp&sid
=l127.

Moynahan, Brian. "Age just a number to All-Star Lucas." 16 August 2011.
http://web.minorleaguebaseball.com/news/article.jsp?ymd=201
10816&content_id=23293290&vkey=news_l127&fext=.jsp&sid
=l127.

Moynahan, Brian. "NYPL notes: Wittels knows highs, lows." 19 August 2011.

http://web.minorleaguebaseball.com/news/article.jsp?ymd=201
10818&content_id=23387002&vkey=news_l127&fext=.jsp&sid
=l127.

Moynahan, Brian. "NYPL notes: Culver keeps even keel." 26
August 2011.
http://web.minorleaguebaseball.com/news/article.jsp?ymd=201
10825&content_id=23730252&vkey=news_l127&fext=.jsp&sid
=l127.

Bus Leagues Interviewees on Twitter

Stetson Allie	Twitter.com/Stetsonallie
Dellin Betances	Twitter.com/DBetances50
Jackie Bradley Jr.	Twitter.com/JackieBradleyJr
Clark Brooks	Twitter.com/clarkbrooks
Cito Culver	Twitter.com/yaboicito
Travis d'Arnaud	Twitter.com/Travisdarnaud
Jim Donten	Twitter.com/ClawDigest
Tug Haines	Twitter.com/TugHaines
Matt Hobgood	Twitter.com/Matt_Hobgood48
Chad Jenkins	Twitter.com/Jenknutz
Coline Kaline	Twitter.com/Colin_Kaline
Jeff Locke	Twitter.com/Jeff_Locke
Mike McDade	Twitter.com/MacDizzleMan
Matthew Neil	Twitter.com/MattNeil86
Jeff Perro	Twitter.com/MiLBClubbie
Craig Wieczorkiewicz	Twitter.com/MWLtraveler
Garrett Wittels	Twitter.com/Gwittels10
Greg Young	Twitter.com/gregyoungjr

Bus Leagues Interviewees on the Web

Bruce Baskin	Baseballmexico.blogspot.com
Clark Brooks	RawCharge.com, Clarkjbrooks.blogspot.com
Tiffany Brooks	brooksbasa.us
Jim Donten	Clawdigest.com
Tug Haines	CasualFan.org
Joe Price	Anthemtour.blogspot.com
Craig Wieczorkiewicz	Mwltraveler.com
Kurt Schweizer	

http://www.facebook.com/groups/107433322624423/

About the Interviewers

Eric Angevine is a co-founder of Bus Leagues Baseball. He is a freelance writer from Charlottesville, VA. His work has appeared at ESPN.com, CBSSports.com, and Baseball America.

Chris Fee is a Western New York correspondent for Bus Leagues Baseball. He covers Triple-A baseball, primarily the International League, and serves as the creator, host, producer, and editor of the Bus Leagues Podcast.

Scott Grauer is a journalism student. He frequently covers the California League for Bus Leagues Baseball. He also writes about the Phillies farm system at Philly Sports Central and co-hosts the Rays Prospects "Future Considerations" podcast.

Michael Lortz is a Tampa-based Florida State League correspondent for Bus Leagues Baseball. He has written for MiLB.com, the Tampa Bay Times, Deadspin.com, RaysIndex.com, and various other websites. He has also done stand-up comedy throughout the Central Florida area.

Brian Moynahan is a lifelong resident of southern New Hampshire. In addition to co-founding Bus Leagues Baseball, he conceived and edited both volumes of *The Bus Leagues Experience* and has contributed to Chicago Sports Weekly, ESPN.com, and MiLB.com.

Tamara Swindler is the Arizona correspondent for Bus Leagues Baseball. She follows collegiate, independent, minor and major league baseball including Spring Training in the Cactus League, Arizona Fall League, and the All-Star Game Events.

17736356R00145

Made in the USA
Lexington, KY
08 October 2012